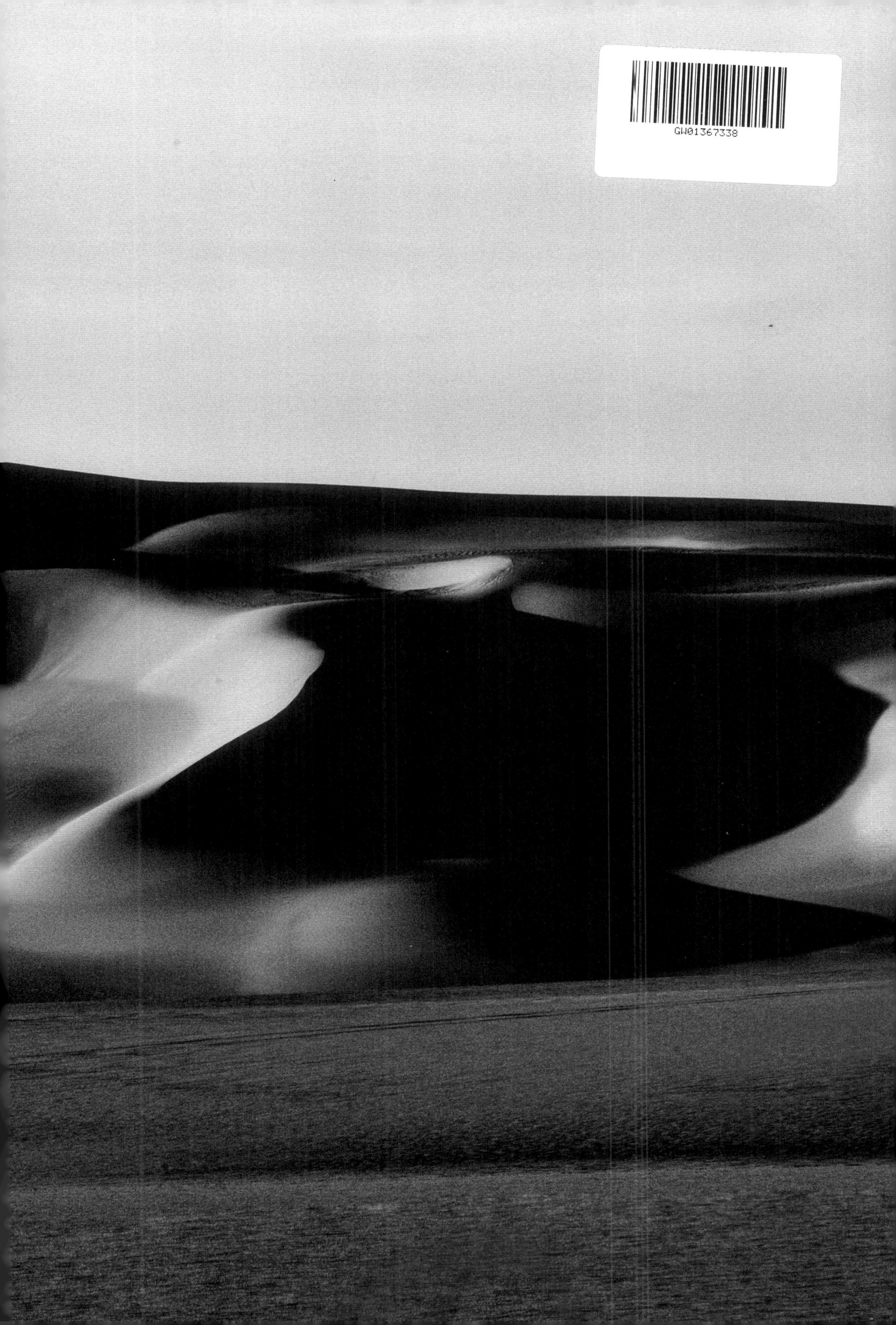

SIWA

SIWA: LEGENDS AND LIFESTYLES IN THE EGYPTIAN SAHARA

ISBN 978-988-19195-0-2

Published in Hong Kong by Haven Books Limited

www.havenbooksonline.com

Copyright © 2011 by SODIC and the individual contributors

Design director: Timothy Jones

All rights reserved. No part of this book may be photocopied, reproduced, transmitted digitally, or translated in any form without the express premission of the authors, photographers and the publisher.

Photographers' credits:

OMAR HIKAL
Pages 4, 10-11, 12, 15, 16, 19, 20, 24-25, 27, 28, 32, 36, 38, 39, 44, 45, 46-47, 48-49, 56-57, 59, 60, 62-63, 71, 72, 79, 80 (top), 86, 87 (top left), 88-89, 94, 96, 97, 100-101, 102-103, 106-107, 109, 119, 122, 124-125, 126, 127 (middle row, right), 128-129, 132 (top), 133, 140

KHALED SHOKRY
Pages 6-7, 8, 18, 22, 26, 30-31, 33, 34-35, 37, 40-41, 42-43, 50-51, 53 (top), 54, 55, 58, 61, 64-65, 66, 67, 68-69, 70, 76-77, 78, 80 (bottom), 81, 82, 83, 84-85, 87 (top right, bottom left & right), 90, 91, 92-93, 95, 98-99, 104-105, 115, 116, 123, 127 (all except middle row, right), 132 (bottom), 136, 141, 142-143, 145

SIWA

LEGENDS & LIFESTYLES IN THE EGYPTIAN SAHARA

RAWAH ALFALAH BADRAWI

PHOTOGRAPHS BY
OMAR HIKAL & KHALED SHOKRY

Haven
BOOKS

Remains of the Temple of Umm Ubayda, near Aghurmi rock in Siwa

CONTENTS

FOREWORD
9   MAHER MAKSOUD

INTRODUCTION
13   RAWAH ALFALAH BADRAWI

REFLECTIONS ON SIWA

20   ABDALLAH BAGHI
28   AZZA FAHMY
34   ROBERTO ROSSELLINI & GABRIELLA BONETTI
44   PRINCESS MEDIHA & PRINCE ABBAS HILMI
52   ISABELLA ROSSELLINI
60   ABDUL HAYY HOLDIJK
72   RANA CHALABI
79   INDIA MAHDAVI
86   SAYED ABOUL KASEM
90   SABRINE EL HOSSAMY
96   RAFIC SAID

INSPIRATIONS FROM SIWA

108   **ART**
       ADEL EL-SIWI
114   **JEWELRY & COSTUME**
       LAILA NAKHLA
120   **DÉCOR**
       AHMED ALI
       ABDEL SALAM GHANEM
130   **CUISINE**
       FEATURING ATEF ABDEL RAHIM

El-Gaari Mountain casts its perfect reflection over Lake Siwa

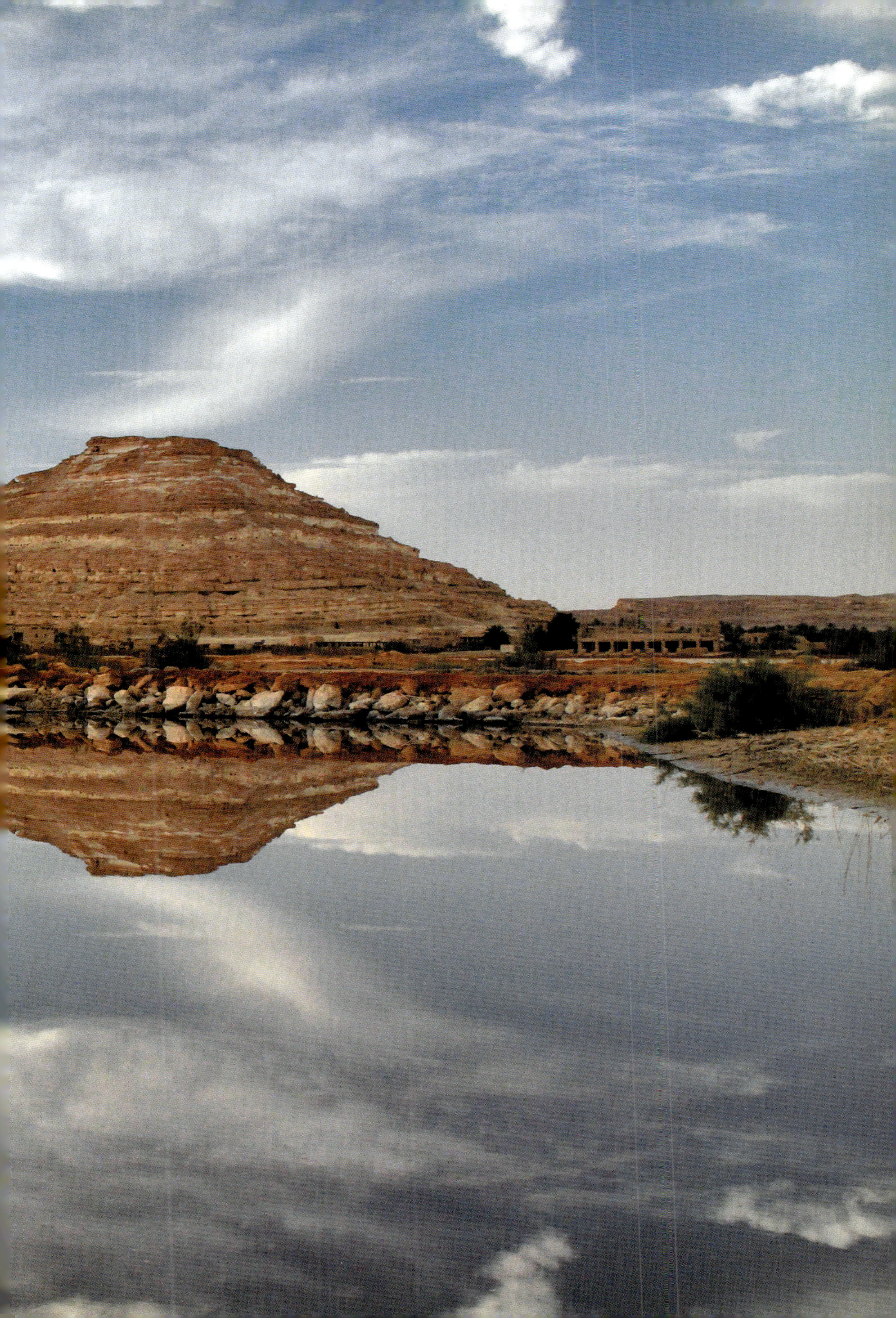

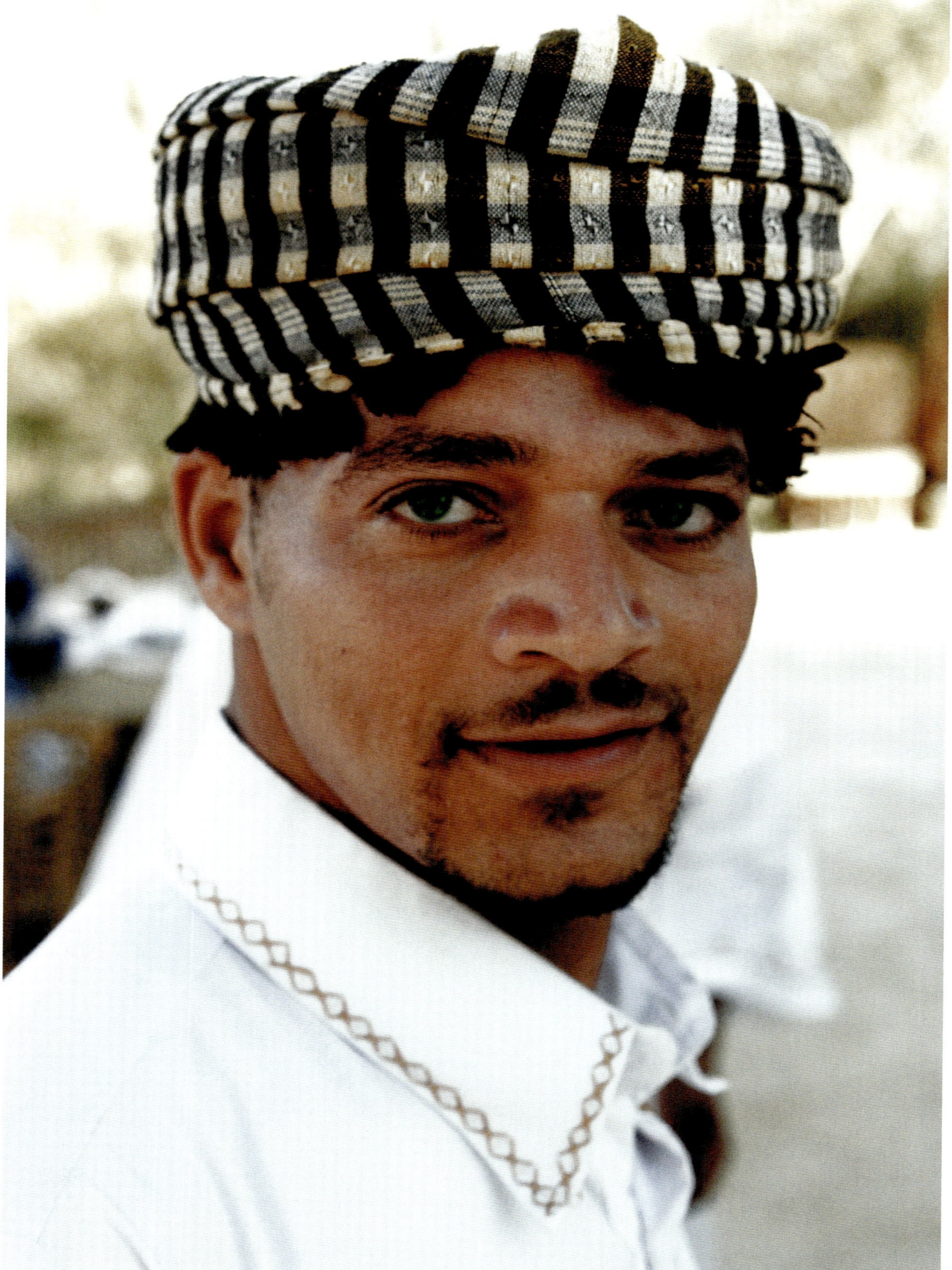

FOREWORD

AS I WRITE THIS NOTE IN MARCH 2011, THERE IS AN OVERWHELMING FEELING AMONGST EGYPTIANS THAT WE ARE IN THE THROES OF A UNIQUE MOMENT OF DESTINY, FULL OF PROMISE AND OPPORTUNITY FOR OUR COUNTRY AND THE FUTURE OF OUR CHILDREN. AHEAD OF US ARE SURE TO BE MANY DAUNTING CHALLENGES AND MOMENTS OF FRUSTRATION AND EXHAUSTION, BUT THE PRIZE WE SEEK IS SO GREAT AND SO NOBLE AS TO BE WORTH EVERY ONE OF THE SACRIFICES THAT WILL HAVE TO BE MADE IN ITS CAUSE. THE PRIZE IS A FREE AND PROUD EGYPT WHERE ALL OF ITS PEOPLE FEEL THEY TRULY BELONG AS EQUALS; WHERE EVERYONE HAS THE RIGHT TO DREAM OF A BETTER FUTURE AND TAKE CONCRETE STEPS TO MATERIALIZE THESE DREAMS WITHOUT CENSORSHIP, INTIMIDATION OR INTERFERENCE.

As proud and captivated as I am with this remarkable revolution, I must candidly and humbly admit that it took me by complete surprise. After decades of political, cultural and social apathy and stagnation, many of us had grown to believe that we were destined to the status quo or, at best, to a narrow band of change, progress and civil-society involvement sanctioned by the system. Over time we became truly convinced of the negative stereotypes of Egypt and of ourselves; we lost hope and the will and confidence needed to restore it.

And then suddenly, the revolution arrived. It was, in every way, deserving of the hyperbolic adjectives used to describe it: *peaceful, informed, united, patriotic, politically astute, proud, pure, brave, organized, selfless* and many, many others. It would be excusable to believe that these words were being used to describe a radically different country and a different group of people! How could this enormous change have come about so quickly and where did it come from? How did the youth of Egypt manage to restore hope and dignity and overcome fear and tyranny? There is clearly a lot going on below the surface in Egypt and, as we have been saying at SODIC for a while now, it really is "time for a different view" of our country and of ourselves. It is time for a full and honest re-evaluation of our strengths, weaknesses and potential; time for us to think in terms of the community as opposed to the individual; time for us to have big, audacious dreams and to plant seeds for projects of transformational scale; and, as a precondition to all this, time to muster all the courage, strength and spirit needed to turn them into reality.

This book embodies much of the positive spirit of this time: it is the product of simple but effective cooperation by a group of self-motivated, talented and sincere people. Both the product of their work and their great spirit deserve enormous praise and respect. This book is inspired completely by the love for Egypt—its vast beauty, diversity and wonder; it promotes tourism and the potential of untapped locations and ideas; and, importantly, it promotes grass-roots development by channelling the sales proceeds to developmental projects in Siwa. We are proud to be part of the making of this book and invite you to reflect on its message of beauty, simplicity and heritage.

MAHER MAKSOUD
CEO, SODIC

Adrere Amellal ecolodge at dawn, on the banks of Lake Siwa

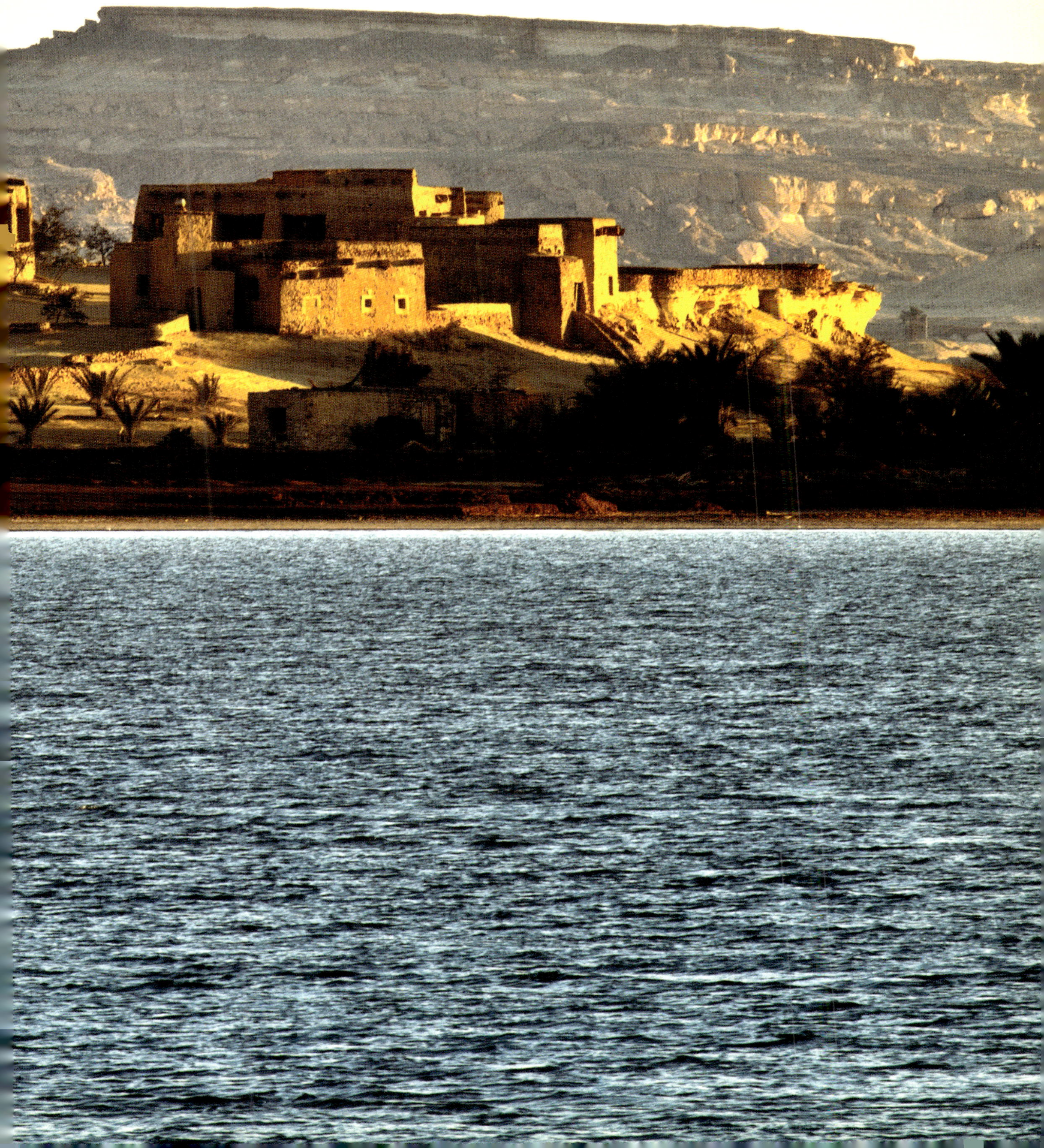

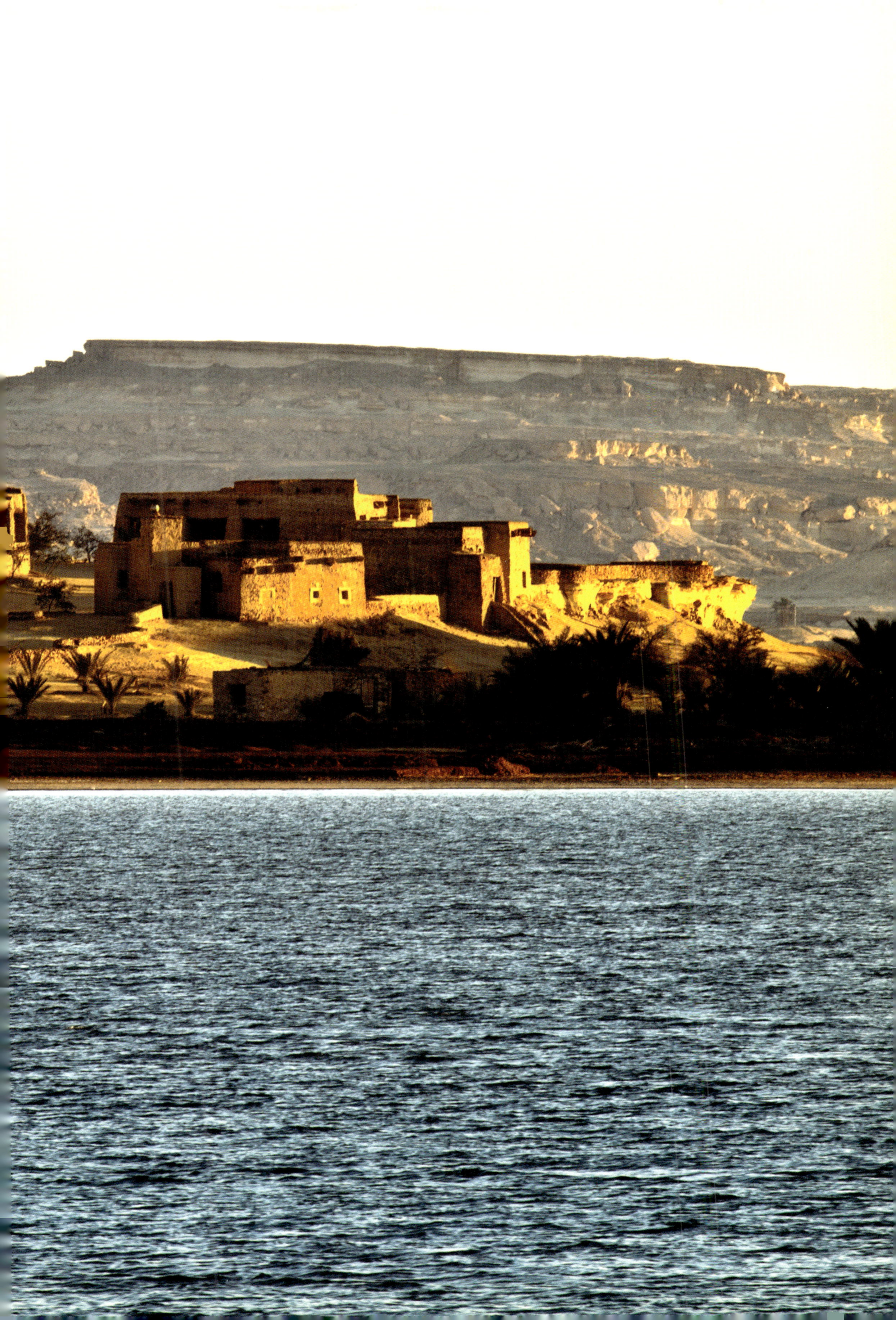

INTRODUCTION

THE SAHARA IS A STRANGE PLACE. THROUGHOUT HISTORY IT HAS BOTH ENCHANTED AND INTIMIDATED ITS VISITORS AND INHABITANTS. THE OPEN STARLIT SKIES, UNMARKED DESERT SANDS AND DUNES, DIVERSE TEMPERATURES AND CONDITIONS, INSULAR TRIBES AND CULTURES, ALL LEND TO A RAW AND PARADOXICAL LANDSCAPE THAT MAKES NO APOLOGIES FOR ITS MOODS OR ITS CONTRIBUTIONS TO HISTORY. EGYPT HAS A CLAIM ON THE EASTERN-MOST TIP OF THE SAHARA AND WITHIN THIS SLIVER OF DESERT LIES A SMALL TOWN WHICH AT FIRST GLANCE MAY SEEM INSIGNIFICANT AND DECREPIT. TO THOSE WHO KNOW IT WELL, HOWEVER, IT IS A STUDY OF LARGESSE IN BOTH LEGENDS AND LIFESTYLES. THIS TOWN IS SIWA.

In a country where people flock by the millions every year to see the Giza Pyramids, pose by the Sphinx, board vessels to visit the Ancient Egyptian sites of Luxor and Aswan, it is no wonder that Siwa has remained under the radar. And perhaps it is *because* it has remained clandestinely nestled in its deep desert surround that it has maintained a mystical star quality among Egyptian towns and cities today. It is almost as if Egypt moved in one direction while Siwa chose to stand very still, and in this deliberate stillness it offers those who visit a credible glimpse into the Siwa of ancient times.

Of course, the fact that reaching Siwa is difficult in itself has distracted many people from making any real plans to visit it. Siwa is an oasis town located between the Qattarra Depression and the Egyptian Sand Sea in the Libyan Desert. It sits on the world's largest sand deposit and has two lakes and hundreds of natural springs. The local population comprises about 25,000 people who have a distinctive culture and language. Siwans are a proud yet cautious people. Bahaa Taher's novel *Sunset Oasis* portrays them as wary of foreigners and steeped in superstition. Today, Siwans are accustomed to seeing tourists walking through the town center and visiting historical sites, and some have managed to create a modest living from that business. Their language—referred to as *Siwi*—is spoken but not written, and etymologically seems to be an unexpected combination of Berber and German.

SIWAN HISTORY & LEGEND

Siwa was a force to be reckoned with in the tumultuous days of antiquity. As the home of the Oracle of Amun—an important God in Ancient Egyptian mythology—with its priests and dedicated temple, Siwa possessed an important spiritual component. When the Persians invaded Egypt in 525 BC under King Cambyses, he made the decision to dispatch a large army to march through the desert to Siwa and raze it to the ground. It seems he held a grudge against the Oracle—perhaps its priests had predicted his failure in Egypt and imminent demise. An army of 50,000 men set out as planned but they disappeared shortly after leaving the Kharga oasis, never to be seen again. Historical texts refer to the soldiers perishing in a violent sandstorm in the Western Desert en route to Siwa.

For those who worshipped Amun, it must have seemed that he had exacted powerful revenge on the foreign army that tried to destroy his temple and relegate his priests to a life of slavery. The disappearance of the army and the death of Cambyses himself shortly thereafter gave the Oracle a certain power. Modern-day explorers have exhausted all the resources at their disposal searching for the lost army of King Cambyses, hoping to discover museum-worthy treasures with their remains. They have found nothing.

he Oracle of Amun rose to true celebrity status in 450 BC when Cimon, the son of Miltiades and a major military leader and statesman from Greece, consulted the Oracle of Amun at Siwa by correspondence as his fleet was attacking Cyprus. The fact that he chose to invoke the Oracle at Siwa instead of Delphi probably had to do with the fact that Egypt was a military base for his Cyprus expedition, and it certainly proved interesting. The Oracle apparently urged the Greeks to turn back. Later, the Greeks learned that the Oracle's pronouncement came on the very same day that Cimon had died in the Cypriot town of Kition. The Ancient World was stunned into silence at the powerful prophecies of the Oracle of Amun. This was the turning point for the Ancient Oracles, as heavyweights Delphi and Dodona would now have to share oracle-related profits with a third party: Siwa. Travelers from all over the world crossed the tough terrain of the Western Desert to consult the Oracle, providing expensive gifts in return for having their questions answered by Amun. Siwa suddenly became the oracle capital *du jour*.

Enter Alexander the Great, who from a very young age was a believer in oracular pronouncements, due in large part to the influence of his teacher Aristotle. When he took the throne at the age of 20 he had two stated political promises: to unite Greece and to conquer the Persian Empire. He delivered on both of these promises. When he entered Egypt, the locals greeted him as their liberator from Persian oppression. At Memphis, the capital of Egypt at that time, he was crowned as a Pharoah of Egypt. In 331 BC he traveled down the Nile through the Delta, ending his tour with Alexandria where he laid the foundation for the design of the city of his namesake by the architect Democrates of Rhodes. Historians believe it was at this point that Alexander made the courageous decision to march his army through the desert for six weeks to Siwa. They would have died along the way had it not been for a fortuitous rainstorm, which enabled them to gather water in tarpaulins and forge ahead. They encountered more obstacles when a sandstorm erased their travel route; so Alexander ordered that they follow the ravens which appeared overhead, believing the birds were probably on their way to an oasis. He was right, and they arrived in Siwa intact and unharmed. Alexander the Great was greeted at the Temple of Amun with pomp and ceremony. He asked several questions publicly and the answers the Oracle gave him confirmed that he was the son of a god, and a successful conqueror. However, he later visited the temple again, and allegedly consulted the oracle privately. The question he asked on that visit remains to this day one of the greatest secrets of antiquity. Though we shall never know what was exchanged between the oracle and Alexander in that private cell, he emerged more confident and determined than ever, and went on to lead some of the greatest military campaigns and conquests in the history of civilization. He died in 323 BC in Babylon, taking the secret of his time in Siwa to his grave. It is said that before he died, he told a friend that he wanted to be buried near the temple of Amun at Aghurmi. Fierce speculation about the location of his final resting place continues to this day.

Since that time, Siwa has consistently captured the imagination of travelers and explorers with investigative fervor; the Oracle of Amun and the tomb of Alexander have inspired particularly avid archaeological obsession. In 1792, an Englishman by the name of W. G. Browne masqueraded as a Muslim Turk in a caravan bound for Siwa from Alexandria. He returned from Siwa without having discovered the Oracle of Amun, but his observations about the oasis—the first of their kind for more than 1,700 years—were published in a book that attracted considerable attention from the London African Association (a members-only club with an agenda of exploring Africa). One of the members of the Association was German adventurer Freidrich Konrad Hornemann, who set out to Siwa after meeting with French general Napoleon in Egypt. His observations on Siwa, which also appeared in book form in 1802, were critical to scientists because in 1811 an earthquake destroyed much of what Hornemann had been able to document. Decades later, another German (Gerhard Rohlfs) was the first explorer to produce careful drawings of the oracle cell at the sanctuary of Amun and to copy all the inscriptions and reliefs on the walls. It was not until 1971 that the temple was recovered from underneath the modern village that covered it, and this was the work of prominent Egyptian archaeologist Ahmed Fakhry. These remains can be seen today, perched on Aghurmi rock, in a visibly fragile state.

longside the intrigue and drama at the Oracle of Amun was the small town of Siwa itself. Siwa was founded in the beginning of the 13th century, and its inhabitants moved to higher terrain by building a fortress to protect them from raiders. In the Middle Ages, Siwa was an important hub on caravan and slave trade routes. The large influential families at that time were divided into two factions: the Easterners and Westerners, and in true Shakespearean form they were arch-rivals for several centuries, uniting only in the face of foreign assaults. The Siwans' insular lifestyle and disdain for outsiders was perhaps the manifestation of life in the fortress, which had only one entrance. Today, visitors can see some remains of this "Fortress of Shali" in the town center. Shali has a very unique structure: travelers have compared it to a beehive, with its *kershef* houses built over levels, tiny windows, thick walls and narrow alleys that block the light entirely. The entire oasis with its lakes, palm groves and trees can be seen from Shali's peak, which today is surrounded by the modern town. By Shali's base are homes and buildings, including the oasis' oldest mosque. This structure, dating back to the 15th century, is currently undergoing careful renovation in a collaborative venture between the Environmental Quality International (EQI) and the Supreme Council of Antiquities.

Siwa came under Egyptian rule in 1820. This union was marred by revolts and discontent in those early days. It was a tense atmosphere for the Egyptian civil servants dispatched from Cairo with mandates to work there, and their stays were usually cut short as very few could bear the exile to Siwa. At the same time, however, it was the first time that Siwans felt safe enough to venture outside the Fortress of Shali, building new homes and businesses outside its walls. It wasn't until 1904 that the Khedive Abbas II visited Siwa—the first sovereign of Egypt to do so since Alexander. The Khedive set out into the desert from Mersa Matrouh by horseback, following Alexander's route. It took him seven days, and the Siwans greeted him warmly on his arrival. He distributed silver and clothing to the sheikhs and

Façade of the famous Temple of Amun, where Alexander the Great consulted the Oracle; he was assured of his divinity and victory, but to this day no one knows what the Oracle revealed to him in private

Remains of the Fortress of Shali, where Siwans lived in protective isolation from the 13th century until they came under Egyptian rule in 1820

arranged a special meal for the poor. His gestures were reciprocated generously: the Siwans donated three springs and land that included the largest spring in the oasis, Ain Qurayshat, later renovated by the King.

Following this historic visit, King Fouad was the next sovereign to head to Siwa in 1928. He did so by automobile from his palace in Montazah, Alexandria. In the short time he was there he toured the antiquity sites, witnessed the *zikr* of the Sufi order, granted amnesty to two prisoners, distributed gifts to the sheikhs and the poor, and instructed the construction of a hospital and mosque. He also sent experts from Cairo to help modernize the agricultural techniques in Siwa. King Fouad showed a genuine desire to help this distant realm of his Kingdom, and the Siwans loved him for it. His son King Farouk also visited the oasis when he took the throne, but it was a very brief personal holiday rather than an official visit.

HOW SIWANS LIVE TODAY

Today, Siwa is a quiet Egyptian protectorate. Agriculture is a large part of its livelihood; it produces wonderful dates and olives as well as internationally coveted extra-virgin olive oil. Indeed, the sight of the endless palm and olive groves interlacing the deep desert landscape is one of Siwa's most startlingly beautiful natural scenes. In the past, unmarried garden labourers, referred to as the *zaggalah*, were a force to be reckoned with in Siwan society. They worked for landowners in feudal style, except they had considerable clout. Siwa is rife with stories of the *zaggalah* dancing parties and gatherings. Today, however, the *zaggalah* community has faded, and Siwan men are active in all kinds of trades from agricultural to small businesses in the town center, while the women stay home or produce bedouin textiles and other native handicrafts to sell to tourists passing through town.

Shali, Siwa's old town, has a bustling central market selling local products. Visitors will often buy colorful baskets (*margunas*), wooden boxes with their distinctive carvings, silk-embroidered Siwa shawls and the voluminous dresses sewn in multicolored threads in the shape of outspread rays of bursting colors, a clear nod to the sun god of the Amun temple. Though Siwa is famous for its intricately engraved chunky silver jewelry, and extravagant colorful costumes, sadly they are no longer produced or worn. Siwan women and children dress in contemporary clothing with engineered fabrics and streetwear more akin to that found in Cairo's neighborhoods.

Even on her wedding day, the Siwan bride has swapped the beautiful traditional costume for the white western-style dress. Her jewelry is standard gold bought outside Siwa. Traditional costume and jewelry, which stands out in Siwa because of its distinctive Berber influence and beautiful designs, is a fading art form for a Siwa in transition, striving now to be part of the larger world around it.

One tradition that has stood the test of time and remains a testimony to the town's deep spiritual and fraternal heritage is the *Siyaha* festival. Drawing from Sufi roots to celebrate the birth of patron saint Sidi

Sulayman, the Siyaha takes place for three days every autumn around a full moon at Mount Dakhrour—Siwa's famous mountain, thought to be haunted by *jinn* or spirits. It is a time for reconciliation, contemplation, the strengthening of ties, and celebrating Allah and His attributes. On the first day, livestock is slaughtered in a central site. Tents are then put up, and cooks prepare simple meals for the community.

The most touching aspect of this festival is the way that all the members of the community sit together side by side for their meals; this gesture emphasizes that they are all equal and united. After evening prayers, Sufis gather to invoke God's name and attributes, praising him in an arrestingly rhythmic chant, referred to as *zikr*. Over the course of the three days the notions of patience, modesty, fraternity and camaraderie are reinforced with every action. The message is simple: believers leave the comfort and familiarity of their homes and families for three days to live this modest communal life, a sacrifice they happily perform for brotherhood and for the higher being, Allah.

INDIGENOUS ARCHITECTURE

Historically, Siwans used a combination of rock salt and clay called *kershef* to build their town. The ancient building technique involved stacking blocks of rock salt from Lake Siwa and using the clay from the bottom of the lake to bind them together. Needless to say, while the resulting structures are visually harmonious with the landscape, resistant to rain they are not. In 1926, torrential rain—a phenomenon that appears every half century or so—dissolved a significant amount of the ancient Fortress of Shali built from *kershef*, and today the 'old town' of Siwa is slowly disappearing.

If the Sahara is a strange and secretive place, then the Siwans are in some senses a reflection of that, and protecting their privacy, traditions, and habitat has become the lifelong work of a few people who care deeply about Siwa, most notably the ardent environmentalist **Dr Mounir Neamatalla**, whose ethos has been to protect Siwa's special resources—and in particular to preserve its unique architecture.

At the base of a picturesque white mountain overlooking Lake Siwa, Dr Mounir lovingly designed and developed an unassuming ecolodge called Adrere Amellal (meaning White Mountain in Berber). His lodge is the reason many people have visited and adored Siwa. Though he did not have a hotel mogul's presumption of "build it and they will come", that is indeed what happened. Except that in Dr Mounir's case, the people who came included prominent individuals who subsequently became repeat visitors. Whether this is a testimony to the ecolodge or Siwa, or both, his accomplishment in such a faraway and some would say difficult place is deserving of recognition. His main property, a luxury ecolodge, and his two boutique hotels in town were all built using Siwa's indigenous materials and techniques.

Sadly, in and around Siwa ancient *kershef* structures are being replaced by hastily constructed inefficient buildings of concrete and steel, in a patchwork of unappealing styles. In a way, therefore, Dr Mounir's properties are a refreshing tribute to the real Siwa that lives off the bounty of its earth.

IN THIS BOOK

Siwa is a town that comes from a mythical time, from the deepest imagination. In this book, accomplished individuals from all over the world step forward to narrate the Siwa of their memory.

Siwa native and desert adventurer **Abdallah Baghi** talks of his birthplace and how the preservation of Siwa's heritage, habitat and people has never been more crucial. His ancestor, Ibrahim Baghi, ruled Siwa from 1697 to 1711, during which time Siwa enjoyed unprecedented peace and prosperity. International jewelry designer **Azza Fahmy** writes on how Siwan costume, jewelry and crafts are designed by women who take inspiration from their surrounding environment. **Abdul Hayy Holdijk**, a traveler on the path of Sufism, takes us on a spiritual journey in his piece, paying homage to the silence and serenity of an ancient terrain. His wife, the artist **Rana Chalabi**, sees the beauty of the Siwan landscape through a painter's canvas.

Actress **Isabella Rossellini** applauds the raw beauty of the ecolodge created by her old friend and college roommate, Dr Mounir Neamatalla. Her brother **Roberto Rossellini** and his wife **Gabriella Bonetti** describe it as an oasis for the soul. **Prince Abbas Hilmi**, whose grandfather and Egypt's ruler the Khedive Abbas II conducted a historic visit to Siwa in 1904, enjoys his finest days with wife **Princess Mediha** at their home in Siwa. Financier **Rafic Said** revels in Siwa's wonder and nature, always keen to return to his house there with his loved ones. International architect and designer **India Mahdavi**, to whom Siwa is a precious and holy place, talks about reinterpreting indigenous architecture, and creating products with local craftsmen and women that utilize the resources of the area. Tabla player and recording artist **Sabrine El Hossamy** feels her music sounds better in Siwa's unpolluted silence, recalling fond memories of playing alongside local Berber bands.

There is no doubt that this quiet oasis in Egypt's Sahara has given so many people across time immeasurable pleasure, peace and comfort. If, in producing this book for charity, we can address some of the shortages that affect Siwa and its people, then we would not only have fulfilled our hopes for creative philanthropy, but also paid tribute to a place which has, for thousands of years, stood strong in the face of calamity and adversity.

It is an honor, therefore, to have our guest contributors participate in this book, sharing their most personal reflections of Siwa. Curiously enough, each one of them describes a unique and different Siwa; because the Sahara is strange that way, and promises never to change if we don't let it.

RAWAH ALFALAH BADRAWI
Sakkara, Egypt
January 2011

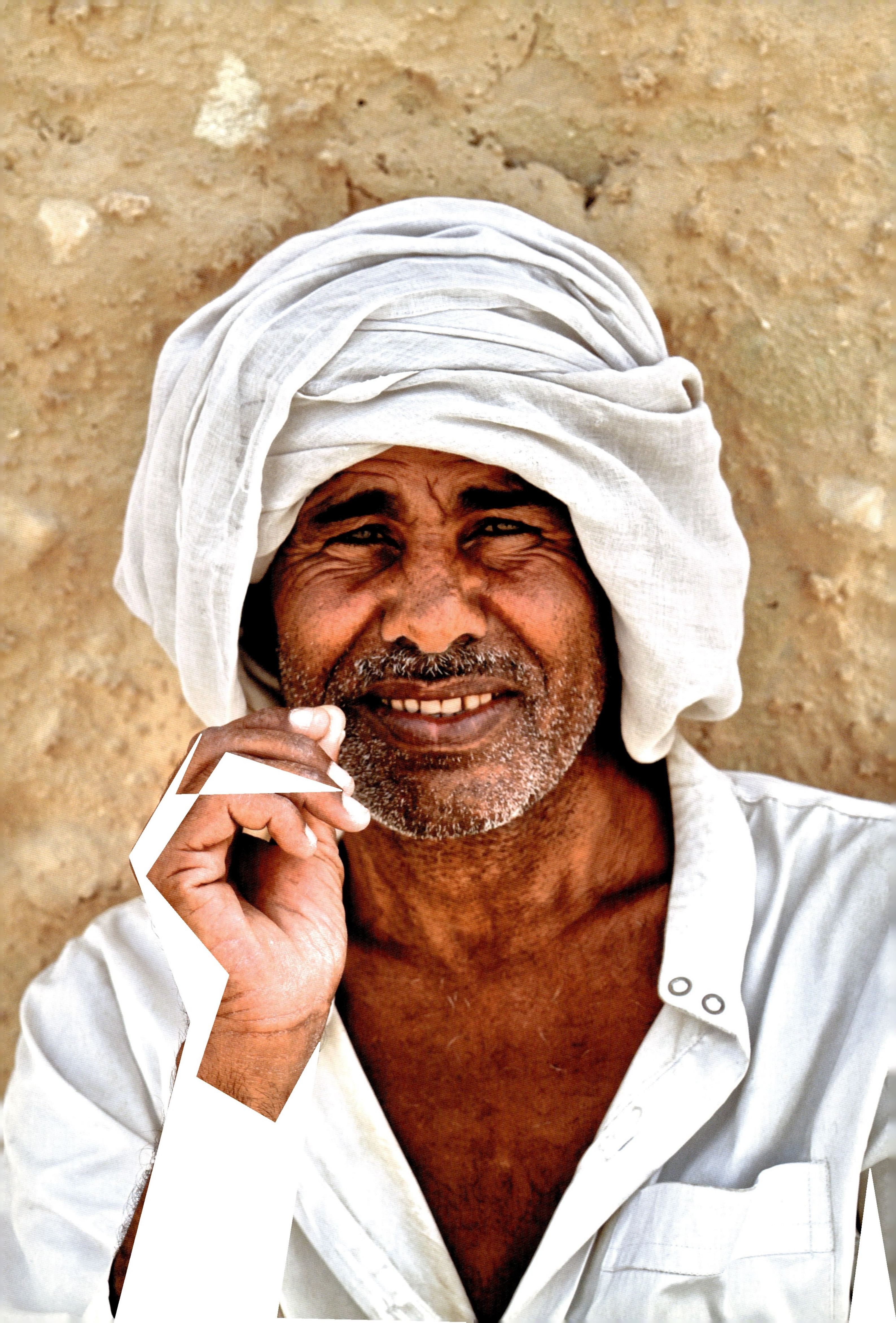

A Siwan man wears white linens and cottons that provide relief from the hot sun (opposite) Women, on the other hand, are wrapped in dark veils that cover them completely (below)

ABDALLAH BAGHI
Head of Siwa's Heritage Conservation Committee, desert adventurer

SIWA IS THE OASIS OF PEACE AND PROSPERITY. THIS UNASSUMING SPOT IN THE SAHARA IS STEEPED IN LEGENDS SO MAGNIFICENT THAT FOR THOUSANDS OF YEARS FAMOUS AND POWERFUL PEOPLE HAVE RISKED THEIR LIVES AND ENDURED ARDUOUS DESERT JOURNEYS TO ARRIVE HERE, AT LAST, TO FIND THE OASIS OF THEIR DREAMS.

How could I not feel honored, therefore, to have been born and raised in the leafy shadows of this green oasis? And in the ten years I spent away from Siwa to pursue my studies, I was haunted by the memory of its palm groves, trees, desert and silky dunes. The nostalgia was so overwhelming, that I made the decision to return, if only to see whether I was chasing a dream that would vanish the moment I arrived. I did not expect to stay long; in the end, I never left. And I'm still here.

The people of Siwa have been my inspiration, just as the oasis itself has been my refuge. In the simplicity of their everyday lives I saw such nobility, fraternal bonds, unity and a deep respect for culture and tradition that dictated the way people lived and worked. They inadvertently created the kind of community one only reads about in books, a utopia almost, where the air is clear, the town is peaceful, and the people are pure. Siwa is a green sanctuary in the middle of one of the most stunning deserts in the world. The Great Sand Sea, with its glistening dunes, is the one place where I feel most at home. This is where I come to be alone, to contemplate my life and immerse myself in the quiet. Yet, this is also a place where I have brought others, to drink some tea, and recount some stories. In the Great Sand Sea, you can tell stories forever.

The oasis has a unique habitat that is in total equilibrium. One of my favorite excursions is to drive through the desert to the deep royal-blue waters of Lake Shiatta, which rises up quite suddenly from the arid landscape, like a jewel. Trees and greenery surround this salty lake; its palm trees offer some of the rarest dates in the oasis. Pink-and-white flamingoes search for marine shrimps as visitors swim in the cool, refreshing water. In contrast, Siwa's sweet-water springs have enthralled visitors since antiquity; they are thought to be restorative and feature often in social rituals. Sadly though, as I write this, I can see how the equilibrium Siwa is so known for is in jeopardy. The punishing forces of modernization, human interference, and the inefficient management of precious resources are all threatening to damage the wonder of this beautiful place.

Special ecosystems around the world are shrinking due to our mistreatment. Siwa is one of those places, and we must unite to preserve this national treasure, so it can be a glorious gift we give our future generations. For many years I worked as a guide in desert safaris, and I found myself escorting heads of state, kings and queens, and global celebrities deep into the Egyptian Sahara. Invariably, we would find ourselves speaking openly and easily, as though we had known each other all our lives. Their praise, happiness and apparent awe for Siwa was startling and exciting. It made me so proud to call myself a son of the oasis. This is indeed the oasis of peace and prosperity, the pearl of the desert, home of the pure: *Siwa!*

Flamingoes fly over Lake Shiatta, a rich eco-system in the middle of arid desert

This Siwan man's ancestry would tell tales of caravan journeys through Africa
A desert safari Jeep (opposite) drives towards the impossible Sahara sunset

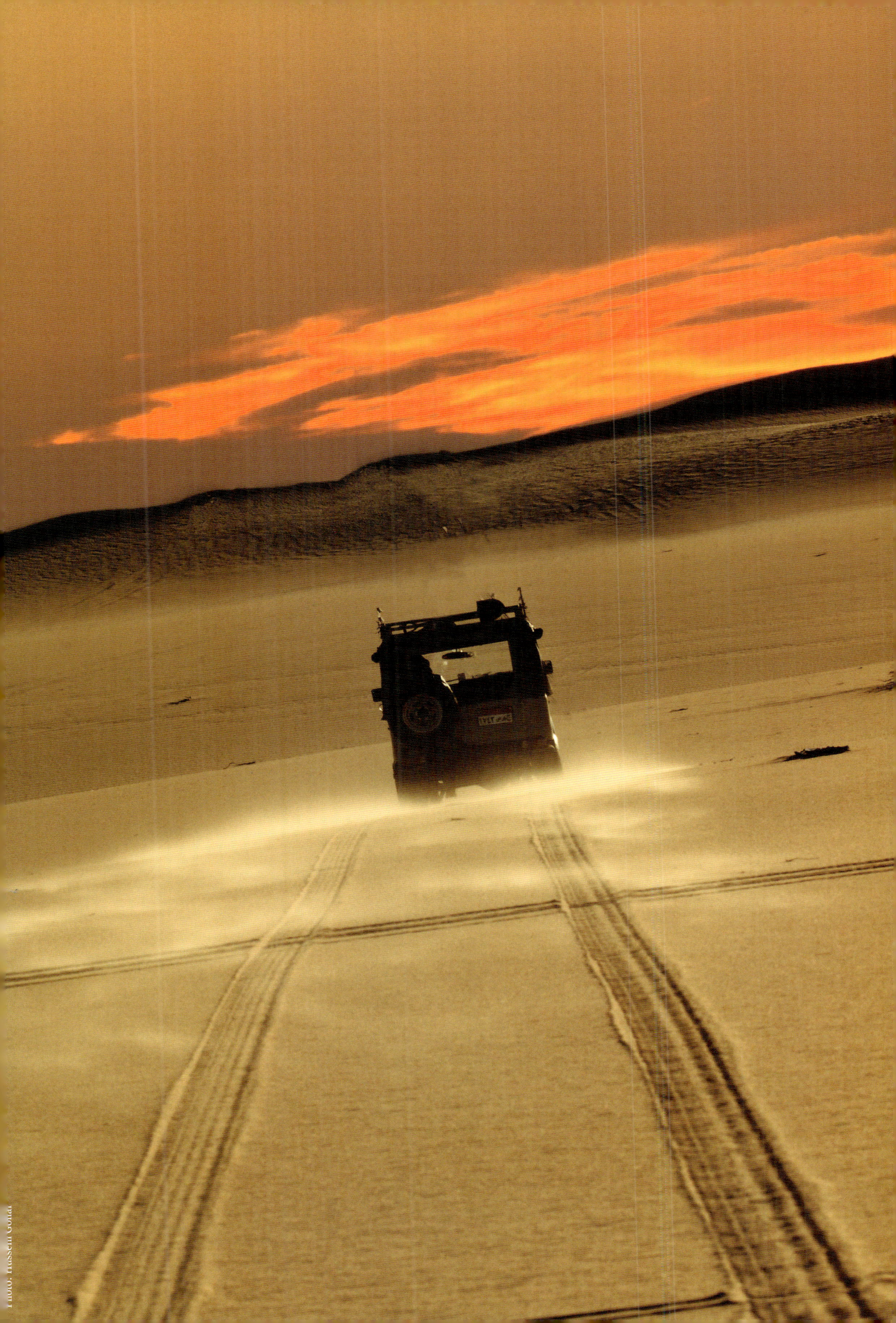

Photo: Hussein Gohar

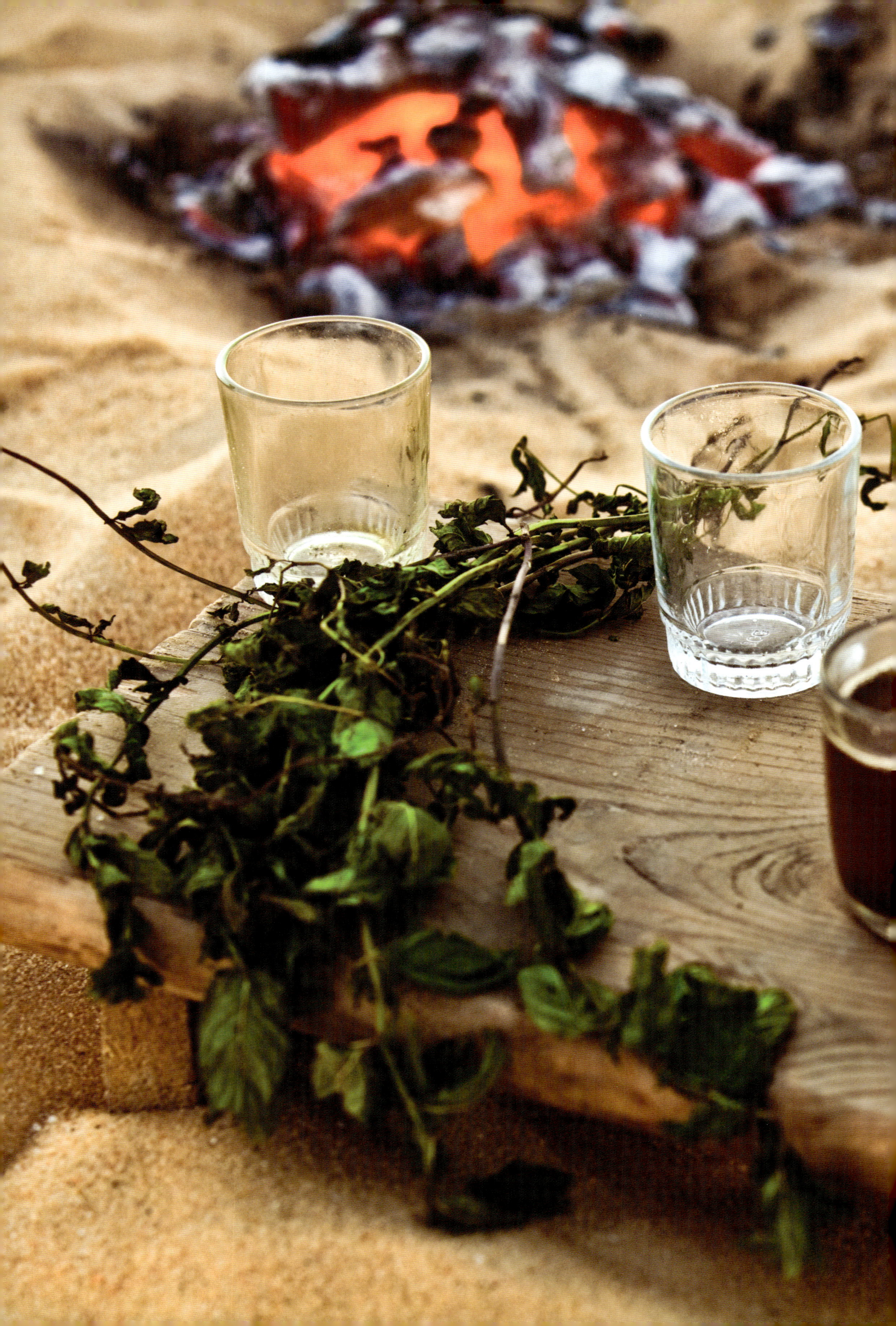

Teatime in the Sahara is a simple affair: hot coal for heating, a plank of wood for placement and fresh mint to serve

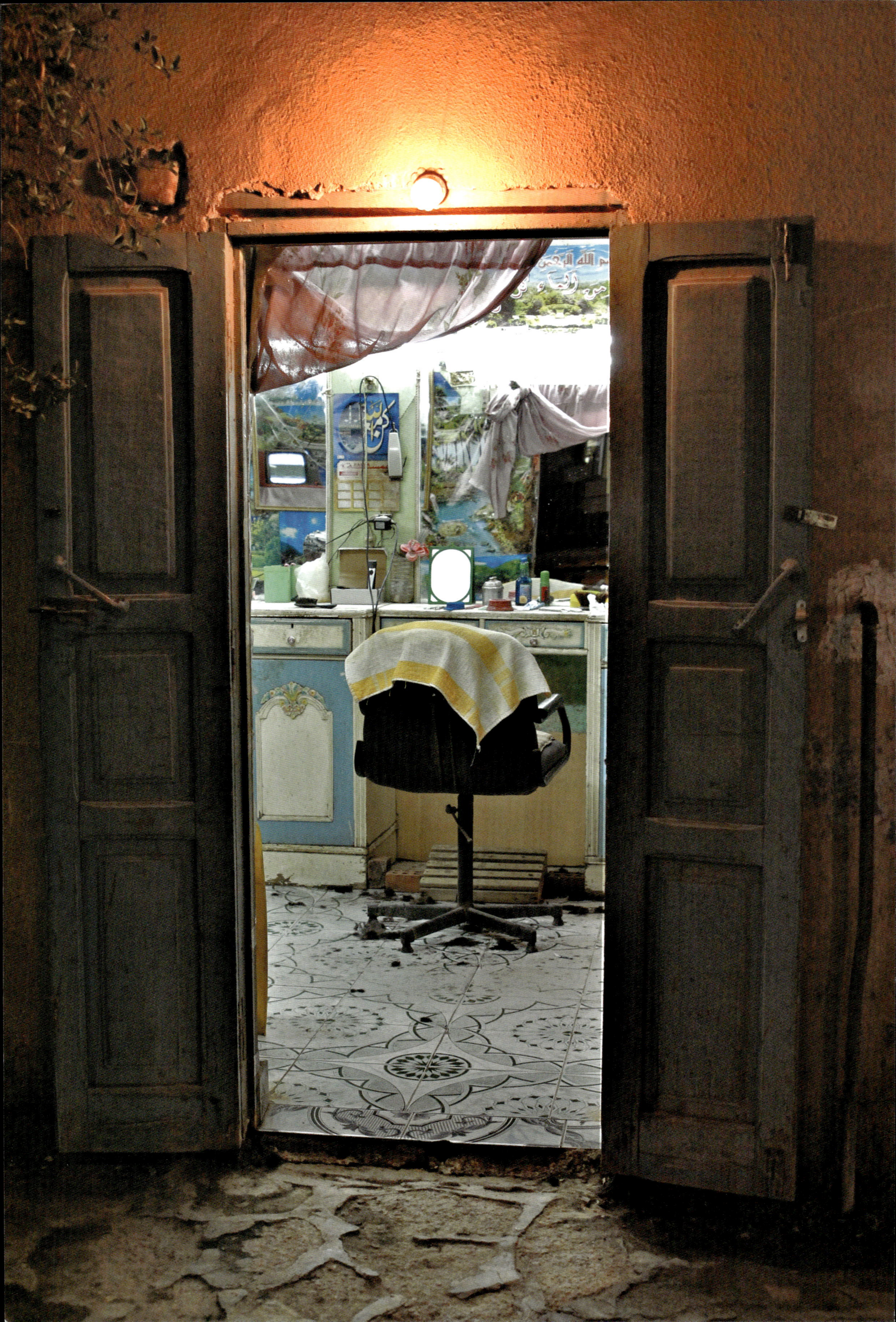

A young Siwan boy standing at the entrance of the Temple of Amun, where his mother offers tourists henna-related services

A typical barbershop in the town center (left)

AZZA FAHMY
Jewelry designer, author

I AM AN AVID TRAVELER. EACH TIME I VISIT A NEW PLACE, I LOOK AT IT THROUGH A COMPREHENSIVE VIEWSCAPE THAT IS THE SUM OF MANY PARTS: NATURE, ARCHITECTURE, COSTUME AND JEWELRY, ARTS AND CRAFTS, HERITAGE AND ANCESTRAL LEGACY, CUSTOMS AND TRADITION. WHEN ALL THESE FACETS ARE PRESENT, THEY COMBINE SEAMLESSLY TO GIVE THE CULTURE ITS SPECIAL IDENTITY AND ITS PEOPLE A WAY TO LIVE THEIR LIVES WITH DIGNITY AND EASE.

This unique oasis town has such an otherworldly quality to it that, despite all my travels, I still feel a strange nostalgia for it. When I imagine Siwa, my mind goes to glorious kingdoms far away… to the highlands of Morocco with its indigenous tribes of the Atlas Mountains; to the famous Ghadames oasis in Libya; and onwards to the Saharan town of Ourzazate, known for its prominent architecture. Walking through Siwa's narrow streets and alleyways, I hear the familiar Egyptian dialect, but I also hear another language with North African roots derived from the Imazighen language. Most Siwans speak both Arabic and a Berber dialect known as *Siwi*. Before 1820, Siwa had one main clan, which played the role of translator between the locals and the traders who came from the Nile Delta and neighboring oases. These traders would buy dates and olive oil in return for various products needed by the Siwans, from apparel to food. For many centuries Siwa's population lived hidden away in the half-lit labyrinth of the Fortress of Shali, rarely interacting with the outside world, capturing the imagination of visitors with its mysterious aura.

As a designer and collector, I am compelled to look at the notion of heritage and culture differently. From an artistic vantage point I see the Siwan woman as the ultimate creator of the Siwan persona. She is the crafter of most of the local products: veils, shawls, costumes, shoes, and of course, glass-beaded necklaces. The choice of colors, materials, and the way in which they are designed are all her choice, a legacy inherited from her grandmother. The design world is the only space where the Siwan woman has complete control and the final say; and she chooses to make it a reflection of her environment. In every sense, she takes her cue from nature. And through the self-discipline she applies to her work, she finds consolation; she will sew her garment and make her jewelry in all circumstances, in every emotional state. This is her odyssey.

There is a large correlation between the colors that the Siwan woman uses in her clothing and the colors of dates in their various seasons. The colors of dates change from when they first appear on the palm tree to a little later on, until finally they are fully mature and take on that deep ochre color. The spectrum is: green, yellow, orange, red, ochre. This artist has instinctively drawn from the colors around her, a testimony to nature's profound effect on her. The sequined threads in traditional Siwan costumes are like sunbursts, reminiscent of the sun rays carved onto the walls of the Temple of Amun. Here the Siwan woman draws on Pharonic and historical influences to complement her choice of colors from nature. This approach reappears in the famous red shoes of Siwa, also sewn with silk thread. Jewelry and costume aside, women in Siwa also create woven baskets (*margunas*) from leather, straw and palm leaves, adding vibrant color. These versatile baskets are synonymous with Siwan household décor, storing clothes, jewelry, money and various pantry items.

I have always been fascinated with the notion that jewelry, costume and other artifacts are a product of their surroundings; a notion I adopted as a designer very early on. From researching the different genres of jewelry in Egypt and writing about them, for example, I learned the great extent to which people were directly influenced by the nature and habitat around them. The Egyptian designer is led by nature and not vice versa. The indigenous jewelry of the Nile Delta and their different techniques, for example, reflect the delicate fertility and agricultural lifestyles that surround the towns overlooking the great River Nile. The azure blue waters laced with lush greenery led the residents of this area to design jewelry rife with detail, expression, and romance. As for desert jewelry, it is robust, with fewer details, reflecting the tough terrain of life in the desert.

Siwa is famous for its silver jewelry, which has features reminiscent of the jewelry seen in neighboring towns in Tunis and Libya. These exquisite pieces were produced in Siwa until the mid-1940s or early 1950s. There were also Alexandrian craftsmen who produced Siwan jewelry. I visited one of them who went by the name Am Amin, a memorable man who took the time to teach his daughter the art of engraving on Siwan silver jewelry. Selecting the semi-precious stones or glass beads that would be combined with the silver, and designing the final style of necklaces was the woman's domain.

What is interesting is that the Libyan town of Benghazi played an important role in supplying Siwa with finished silver components used in stringing necklaces. This was mostly a result of shared family ties and a direct trading route between the two towns. It is a real shame that most of Siwa's antique jewelry and costume has been smuggled out of Egypt and can no longer be seen today. It would have been entirely befitting to view the arsenal of Siwan jewelry and costume in a museum space in Siwa itself, so that both visitors and the local community could appreciate and marvel at the sensitive workmanship of the past. One of my personal heroes is famous Siwan jeweler Gabgab, whose work inspired me tremendously during my due diligence around the country. Gabgab started his career as an ironsmith, then settled into jewelry making in the first half of the 20th century. His pieces are distinctive in their artistic proportions and interesting motifs. He stopped producing jewelry at the beginning of World War II, when the recession and supply shortages made it difficult to work. Sadly, he is no longer with us, nor did he succeed in passing on his trade and artistry to a new generation. With the disappearance of these old masters, as well as the work they created, there is a hollow space where a celebration of Siwan antique heirlooms and treasures should have been.

This small, isolated and introverted community, where even entering a Siwan home seems a virtual impossibility, intrigues me. Yet, the women within these forbidden walls are able to produce items of such beauty, taste, and exquisite originality. It is as if they compensate for their limited interaction with the outside world by creating a magical one of their own through expressive, unbridled design. Even the way the traditional Siwan woman grooms herself turns heads, with her colorful costume, chunky jewelry and her long thick hair braided in several small plaits. She seems a creature from a romantic world one reads about in books—like a traveler from the land of the Berbers of the Atlas Mountains perhaps, or a reincarnation of the Pharonic women engraved on the walls of the Temple of Umm Ubayda. The men and boys typically keep their hair closely shaved; their daily tasks mainly revolving around buying all the household goods and keeping the family supported.

The Siwan woman rarely leaves the house; if she does, it is usually to attend a wedding, birth or funeral. She is enigmatic in every way, and only in recent years did she start to wear the *burqa* when out in public. We see her on the street or atop a donkey cart, her famous Siwan veil leaving half her face exposed to look out at a sliver of the world around her. This veil is of the same material and embroidery that I saw when I first visited Siwa 45 years ago. For as long as she remains hidden behind her clothing and the confines of the conservative world she lives in, few of us will ever really know the extent to which she is an accomplished designer, matriarch, teacher and survivor.

I first visited Siwa in 1966, and I was immediately captivated by this town that made me feel like I was flung in a bygone era, its people unspoiled by urban life, protective of the customs and traditions, deeply committed to the preservation of their identities and privacy. After that initial visit I returned three more times, and each time I would see more unpleasant influences of urban life outside Siwa damaging the special fabric of society and culture. The Siwan persona is slowly disappearing, as it tries to haphazardly emulate the behavior and tastes of larger Egyptian towns and cities. I am heartbroken to see a culture that stood its ground for centuries eroding as surely as the Fortress of Shali or the Temple of Amun, bit by bit, with the passing of time.

I yearn for the old Siwa of my memory, the Siwa I saw and loved in the 1960s, the Siwa that personified authentic culture and history. I hope that we can help preserve what remains from this ancient, proud, and beautifully provocative culture.

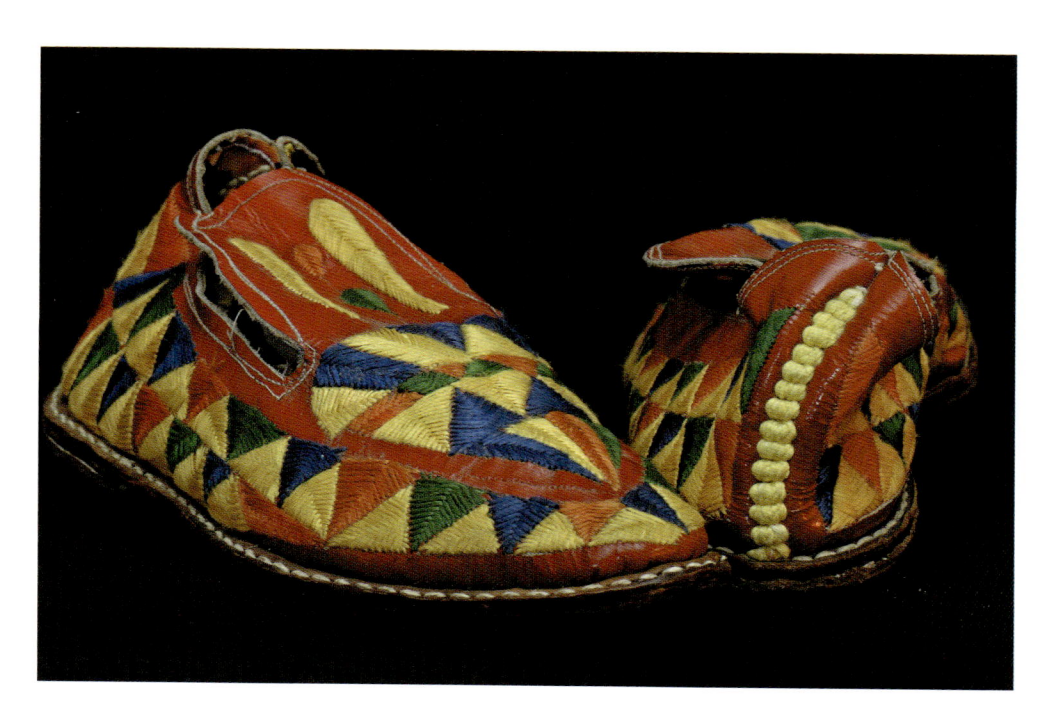

From Azza Fahmy's private collection:

Traditional stitchwork featuring nature's colors (top)

Vintage silk-embroidered shoes

Vintage mascara case

Detail of vintage mascara case

Cuff of a traditional embroidered legging (opposite)

31

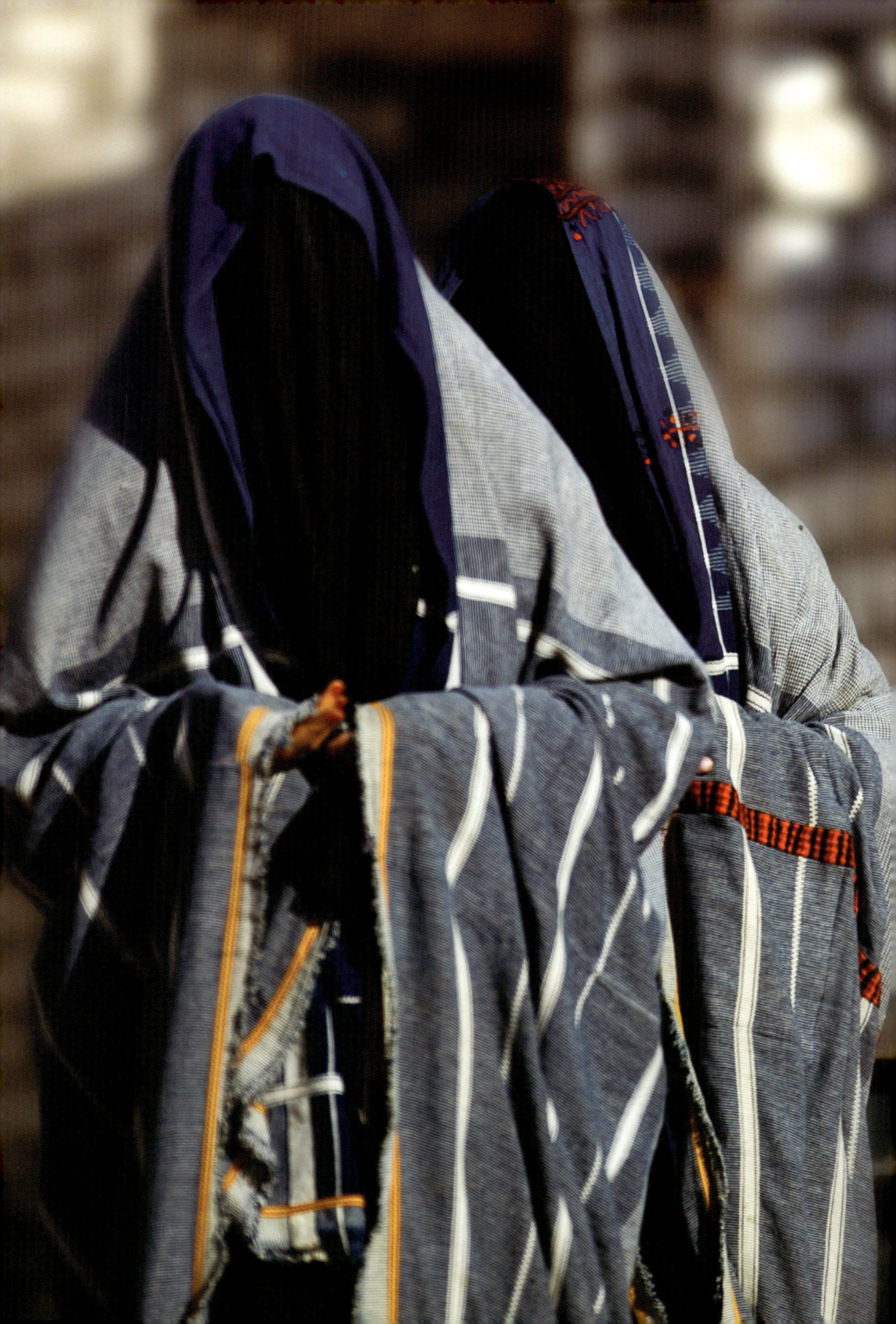

Married women in Siwa are fully covered, their distinctive veils sewn with traditional fabric and embroidery

Traditional woven-straw basket known as "marguna" (top)

Detail of a vintage embroidered bridal dress from Azza Fahmy's collection

A tourist in Siwa wearing Azza Fahmy jewelry; her designs are distinctive with a hint of nostalgia. Here, Arabic prose is engraved on chunky silver pieces.

Traditional Siwan jewelry inspires Azza Fahmy in her own designs (opposite)

35

ROBERTO ROSSELLINI & GABRIELLA BONETTI
World traveler, diplomat

EVERY TIME WE TRAVEL TO SIWA WE GO BY CAR, A LONG TRIP OF ABOUT NINE HOURS. THE ROAD FRAMES ONE OF THE MOST ARID AND UNWELCOMING AREAS IN THE WORLD: THE FLAT, STONY AND DESOLATE QATTARA DEPRESSION. YET WE UNDERTAKE THIS DIFFICULT JOURNEY AS THOUGH IT WERE A SPIRITUAL PILGRIMAGE. WE TRAVEL TO SIWA IN SEARCH OF A HIGHER STATE, OF THAT COVETED SENSATION OF BLISS.

And this is exactly what we experience when, finally, the oasis and its lake surge out of the emptiness. Upon arrival at this sanctuary, we are infused with a profound sense of serenity, calm and wellbeing. Beyond the lake, a new kind of desert emerges: the immense Sahara with its great dunes of fine sand. Here is one of the most spectacular sites in the world, entirely grand and arresting in its silence.

On the bank of the lake, set between oasis and desert, arises Adrere Amellal, Berber for 'White Mountain'. A magnificent ivory mountain that shimmers in the Sahara sun, it stands proudly, in captivating contrast with the cool waters around it. Underneath its slopes thrives a magical world, entirely mythical in quality.

We think of it as an oasis within an oasis; the bountiful epicenter where pleasure knows no bounds. This enchanted spot, created by Dr Mounir Neamatalla, is more than a conventional luxury hotel. It is a palace in the desert, with an otherworldly feel; and in this unique realm the desert itself is Master of Ceremonies. With its refined sophistication, Adrere Amellal defines the notion of elegant simplicity. The light bulb is replaced by candles and moonlight; engineered furniture is set aside as chairs, doors and tables are created from nearby palm trees. And in the evenings, the total quiet and clear night air lulls us into the most perfect sleep.

Once in Siwa, we always find ourselves moved by the sheer scale of the majestic desert, the living beauty of the lush date and olive groves, the blanket of stars overhead that are never obstructed, and the celebration of nature in its purest form. Within the realm of Adrere Amellal, however, it is our spirits that are rejuvenated and lifted.

They remain in that higher state, that reverent bliss, for quite a while afterwards—despite the long ride home, and despite ourselves.

White Mountain, or as they call it in Berber "Adrere Amellal", possesses a unique, almost mystical quality

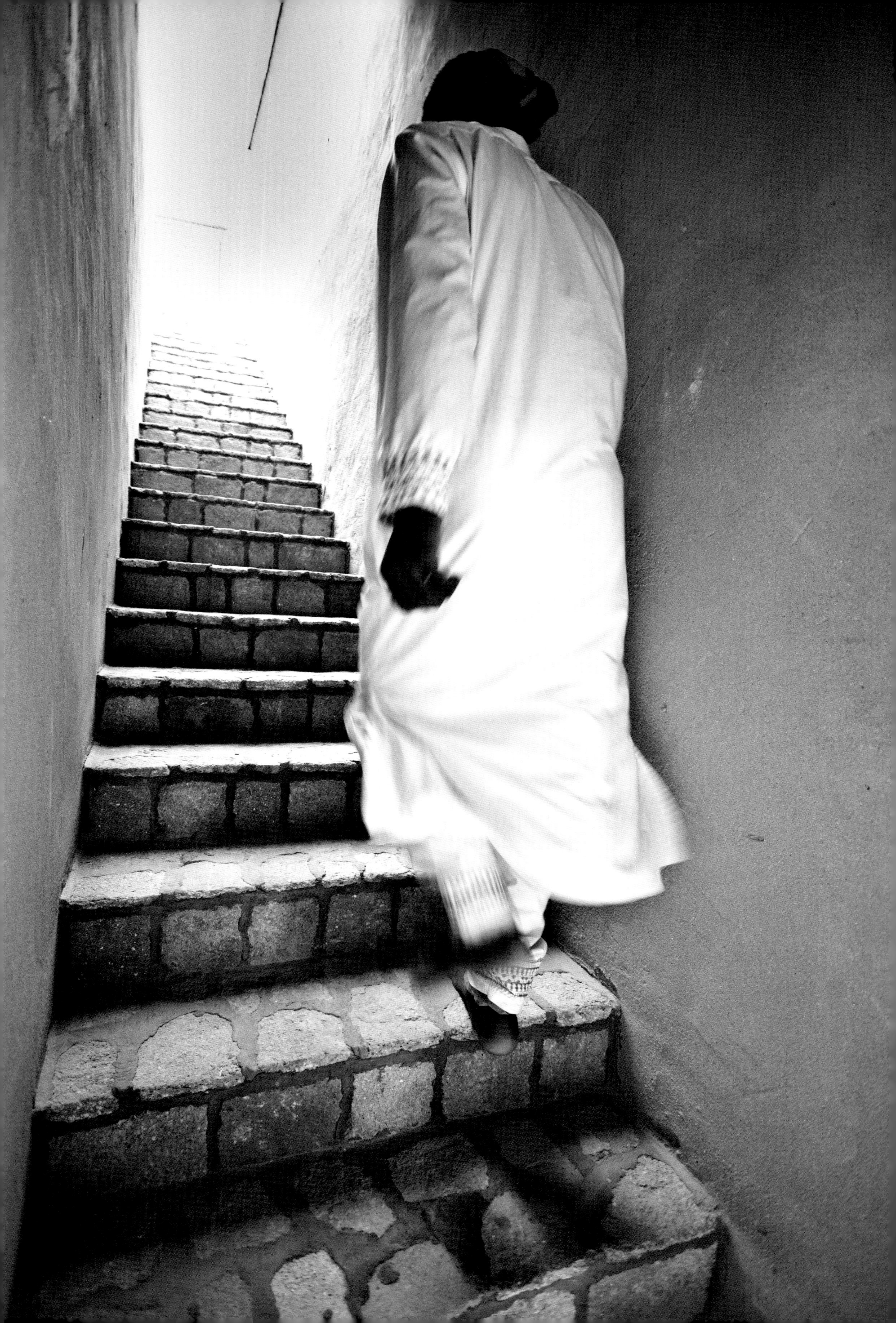

A Berber staffer at Adrere Amellal (left) disappearing quietly up a steep staircase
A fireplace and bedouin rugs keep Adrere Amellal's lounge cozy on a cold winter night

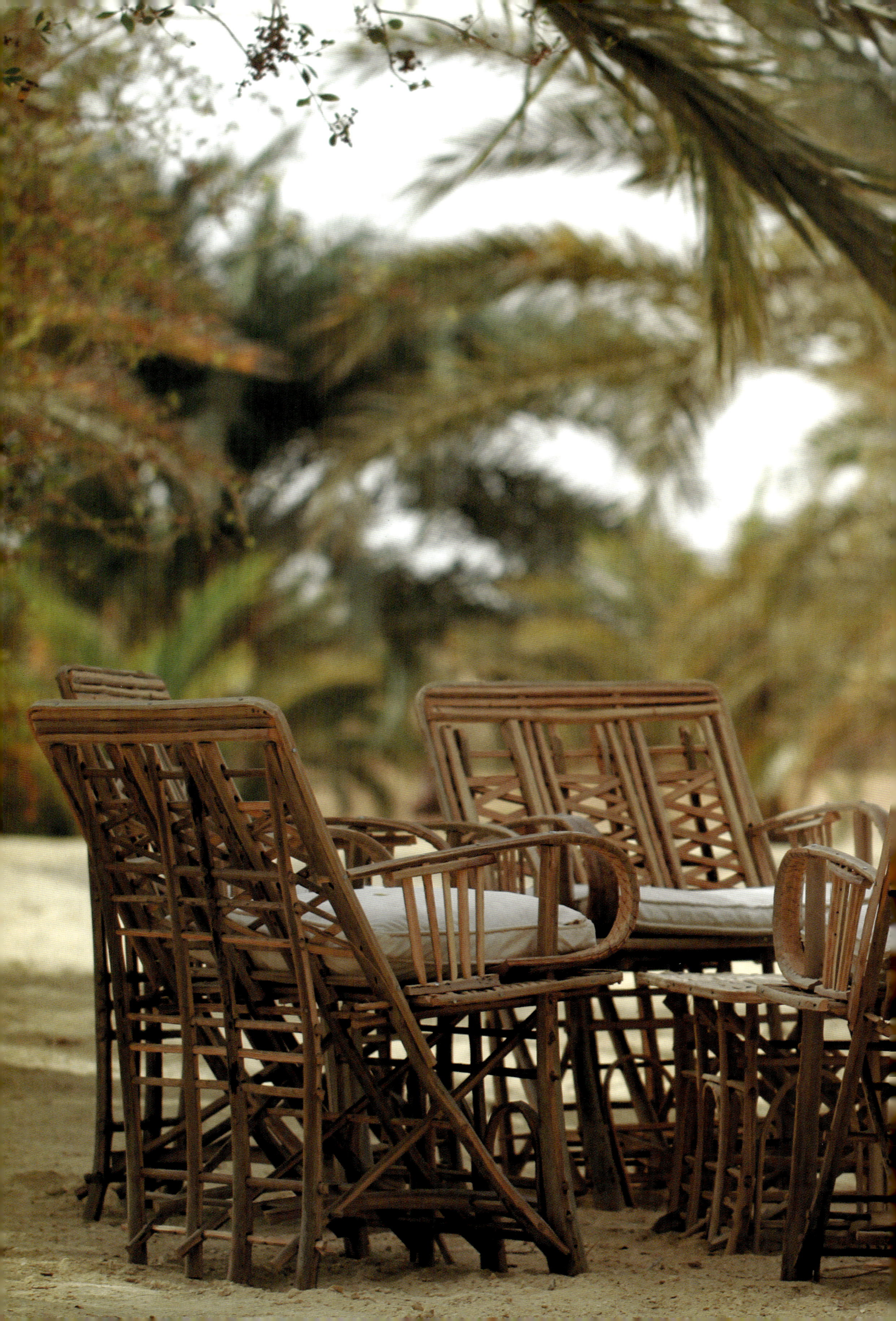

Poolside at Adrere Amellal, chairs and tables made from palm trees beckon under the cool shade of the leaves

الجلسة البدوية ↑
SIWAN SATTING

In the center of town, a medley of services are offered to visiting tourists, including bike rentals, Bedouin textiles and oriental rotisseries

BIKES for rent
دراجات للإيجار

CYCLE For Rent

دراجات للإيجار

Princess Mediha & Prince Abbas Hilmi
Siwa residents

We fell in love with Siwa about 15 years ago and continued to return on a regular basis, having decided to search for a suitable location to build a house. It took us many years to realize our dream, but we eventually found the land we wanted and together built the house that we live in today. The transition from dream to reality was occasionally difficult, but we are delighted to have made the effort, as now we are more attached to Siwa than ever.

When we embarked on developing our property, we tried to respect the surrounding environment. As a result, our buildings are constructed using *kershef*, in the local tradition. We use solar energy to procure electricity for lighting, ceiling fans, refrigerators and even a freezer. We never use pesticides or chemical fertilizers in our garden, and tend to our own livestock.

However, in recent years reinforced steel and concrete buildings have been going up in the heart of town. Town electricity is used to light up the mountain, Gabal Mawta, and incoming roads, detracting from the legendary beauty of the night sky. Pesticides and chemical fertilizers—although officially banned—have made their way to many gardens, causing significant pollution in the lakes. The biggest curse comes from the illegal drilling of wells. The oasis is drowning in brackish drainage water. Some of our olive trees have been affected and are dying.

The strange thing about Siwa is that in all the years that we have been here we have never seen but only heard the mooing of bovines. By contrast, when we visited other nearby oases, it gave us so much pleasure to look at the animals grazing in the fields, enjoying the sun, then returning home at dusk. After enquiries in town, we discovered that the custom is to keep them hidden from view to prevent the evil eye. We suspect this may be a pre-Islamic tradition, but it certainly sheds light on the role of superstition in this society. On another occasion we took a trip with some friends to the Gara Oasis. There we met some young boys with their donkey cart. We stopped to chat and asked them playfully, "What is the name of your donkey?" They laughed hysterically and eventually answered "Izir", which means donkey in Siwi. It dawned on us that they found that the idea of naming a donkey quite ridiculous, though donkeys play a very important role in Siwan daily life.

This is what led us to developing the idea for Siwa's annual "Donkey Day". Locals are invited to submit their donkey to a medical check-up. Winners receive a monetary prize and accessories for their donkey. The objective was to encourage the Siwan community to take better care of the donkey and get into the habit of giving it a name as well. We were pleased to see the villagers rally around the event, and the prize giving is always an exciting moment. For the past three years, Brooke Hospital for Animals has recorded each equine's condition and allocated the prizes according to the individual condition of the animals. Fortunately, Brooke also visits Siwa every fortnight in order to administer medical services to the equine animals and educate the local community.

We love Siwa in every season. Even during the very hot summer months, which can be quite extreme in the desert environment, we climb to the roof of our house and admire the most fabulous sky. It is a place of magic and mystery. We pray that it might be preserved.

Gabal El Mawta ("The Hill of the Dead") is an ancient burial site that has been ravaged by tomb raiders throughout history; the older tombs here date from the 26th Dynasty and Ptolemaic period

A child goads his donkey to move faster, a familiar scene in tribal and rural Egypt

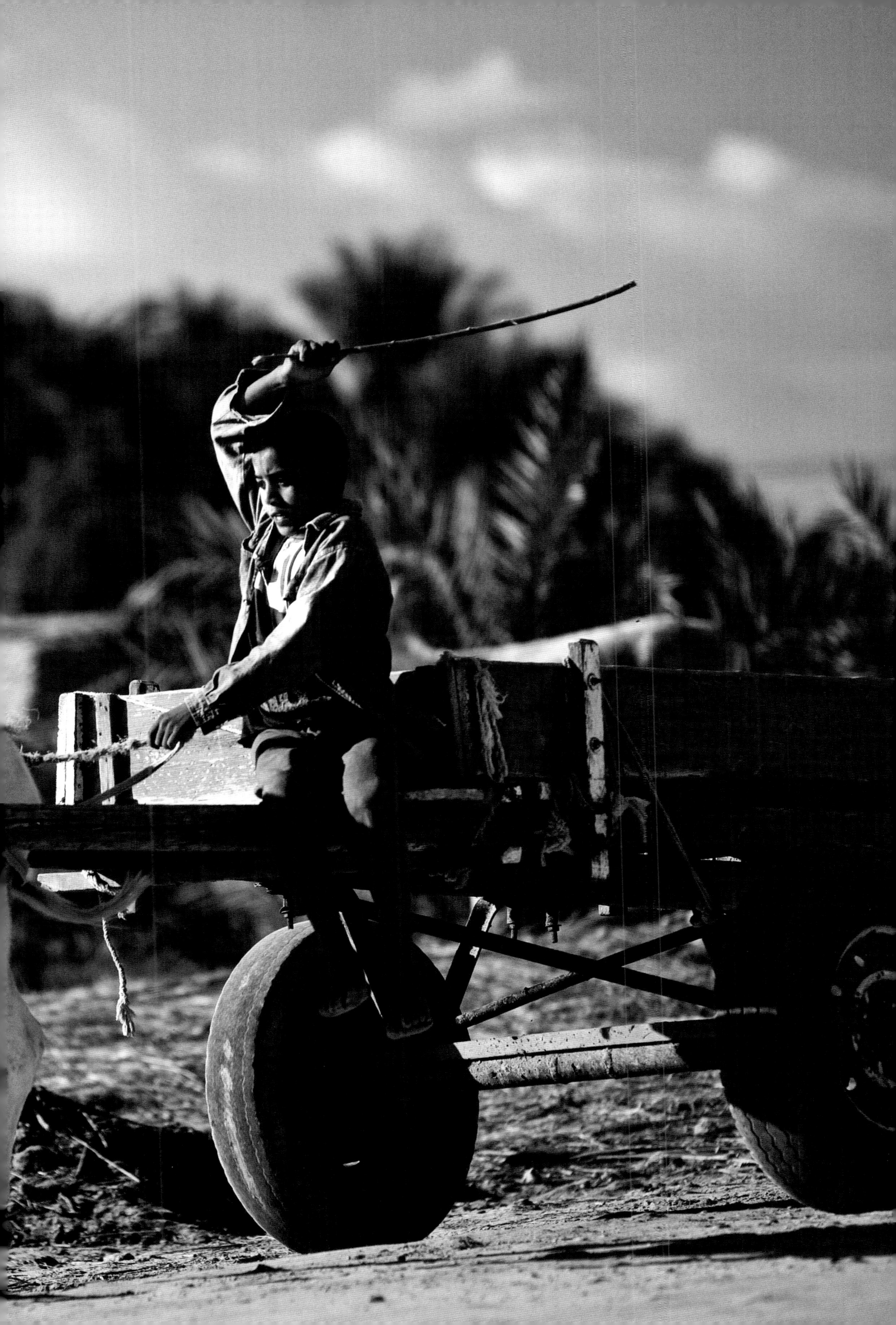

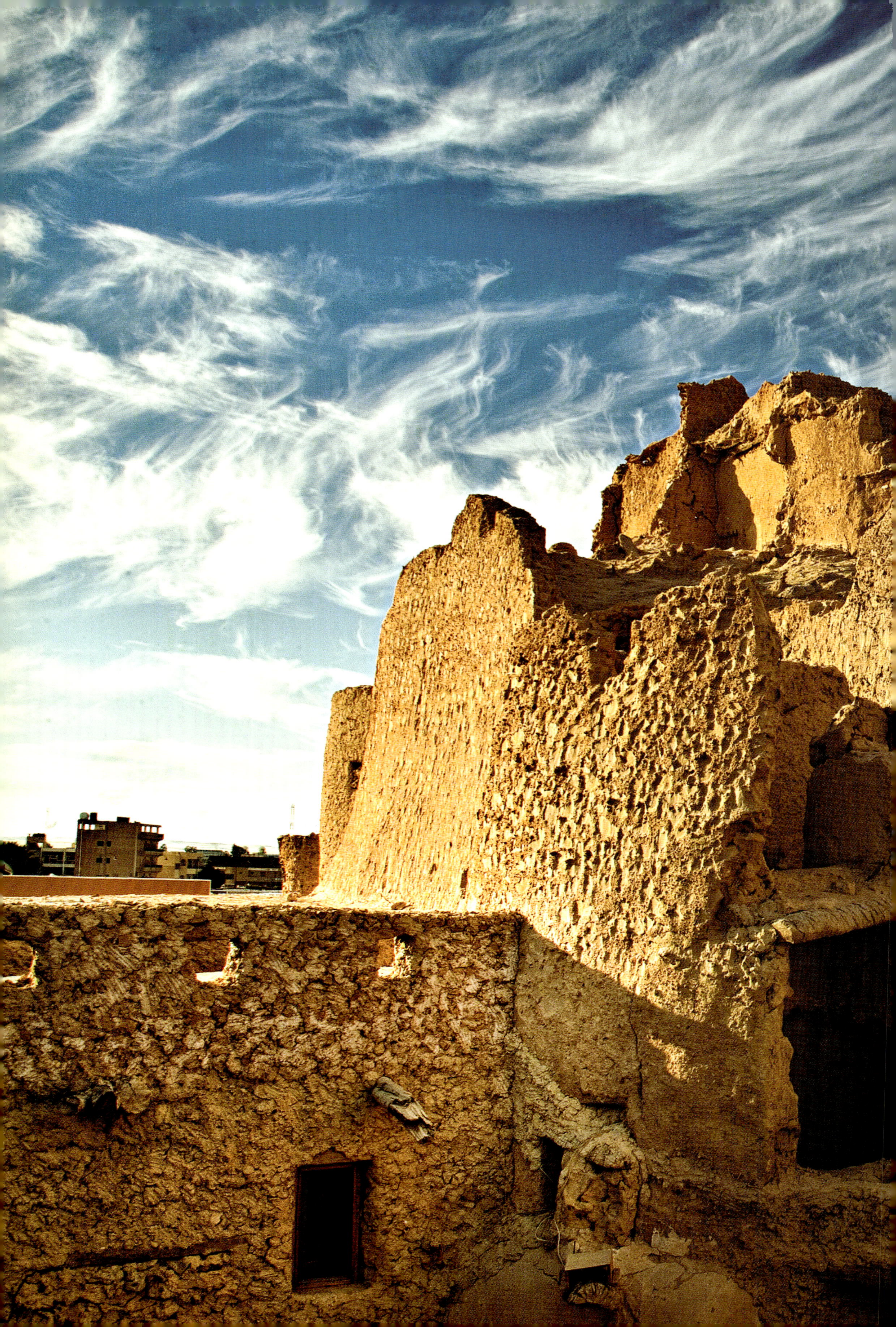

Detail of the disintegrating Fortress of Shali, a curiously shaped ancient town that appears like a beehive with its low ceilings, narrow alleyways and tiny windows

A fruit and vegetable vendor in the town center works after hours in a makeshift stall

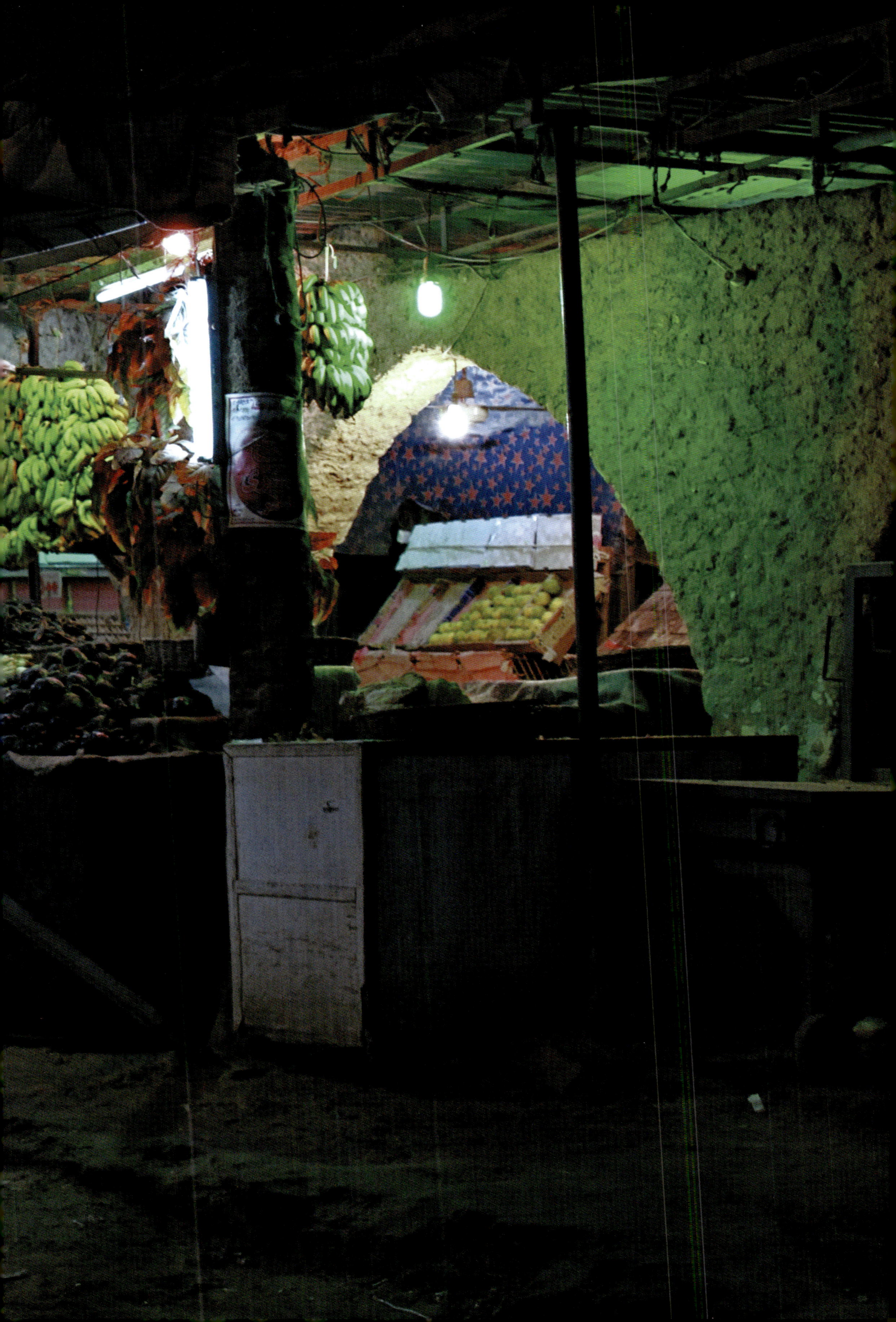

ISABELLA ROSSELLINI
Model, actor, filmmaker
(here with Dr Mounir Neamatalla

NO ONE WOULD BELIEVE ME IF I TOLD THEM THAT ONCE UPON A TIME I WAS THE ROOMMATE OF MOUNIR NEAMATALLA. BACK IN NEW YORK, WHEN HE WAS STUDYING FOR HIS DOCTORATE IN ENVIRONMENTAL STUDIES AT COLUMBIA UNIVERSITY, WE SHARED AN APARTMENT IN LITTLE ITALY WITH OTHER FRIENDS. MOUNIR WAS ALWAYS THE KINDEST, MOST ELEGANT MAN—A REAL GENTLEMAN. HE HAD A REFINEMENT THAT SEEPED INTO EVERYTHING HE DID. HIS WORK IN SIWA EMBODIES THAT PERFECTLY.

I was thrilled to have a chance to visit Siwa some years back, and even more thrilled to have Mounir as my host and guide. Touring the ecolodge he built on an enchanting spot, he explained to me the idea behind its simple elegance. "I wanted to recreate and experience the luxuries of 2,000 years ago," he said. It made so much sense that the quiet, clear skies, pure air, natural light and organic food would be considered luxuries because they are so incredibly hard to find today, even in the most glamorous of cities.

One evening, we had dinner in a room that had a medieval, oriental feel. It was lit with hundreds of candles that cast the most perfect light on our tables. Its walls and ceilings were made with tiles encrusted with mineral salt from Lake Siwa. The candlelight bounced off the salt crystals so that it seemed like the room was glistening, effervescent almost. The tables were sumptuously set up with white tablecloths made from heavy flax that draped all the way to the floor to trap the heat that the thoughtful staff had created at our feet using coal braziers. After the hot Sahara days, desert nights are cold and chilly, so these simple ways of keeping us warm and cozy gave us so much pleasure.

I have eaten so many great meals in my life and in so many parts of the world, yet the food I ate in Siwa stood out. The vegetables and fruit were so fresh and full of flavor; a delicacy in their own right. The organic herb and vegetable farms around us, the palm groves, were all cultivated to put the food on our table, which was cooked with surprising originality. The olives and dates in Siwa are in abundant supply and very special, so food cooked with their essence appeared often in mealtimes, but always in different ways. I remember eating a delicious dessert: a soufflé of dates. I had never had a dish like that before and I *still* think about it. It was so good!

At the end of our exquisite dinner, I walked out to follow the trail of gas lanterns on the sand that led the way to my room. I looked overhead and without electricity I saw the sky in a way I had never experienced before. It was shocking and bright—it was as if I were seeing it for the very first time, with its endless stars and galaxies. I felt like I was in a different era, thousands of years ago actually. This was the ancient Siwa that Mounir wanted to bring back to life. I felt regal in its presence, like a Roman emperor!

Only the soft glow of candlelight illuminates Adrere Amellal in the evenings
Adrere Amellal's date soufflee, immortalized by Isabella Rossellini, is served piping hot in stone earthenware

Photo: Bernard Touillon

53

Salt votives on a dining table at one of Adrere Amellal's nearby signature villas
Gathering lanterns at sunset to mark pathways at the ecolodge before night falls (right)

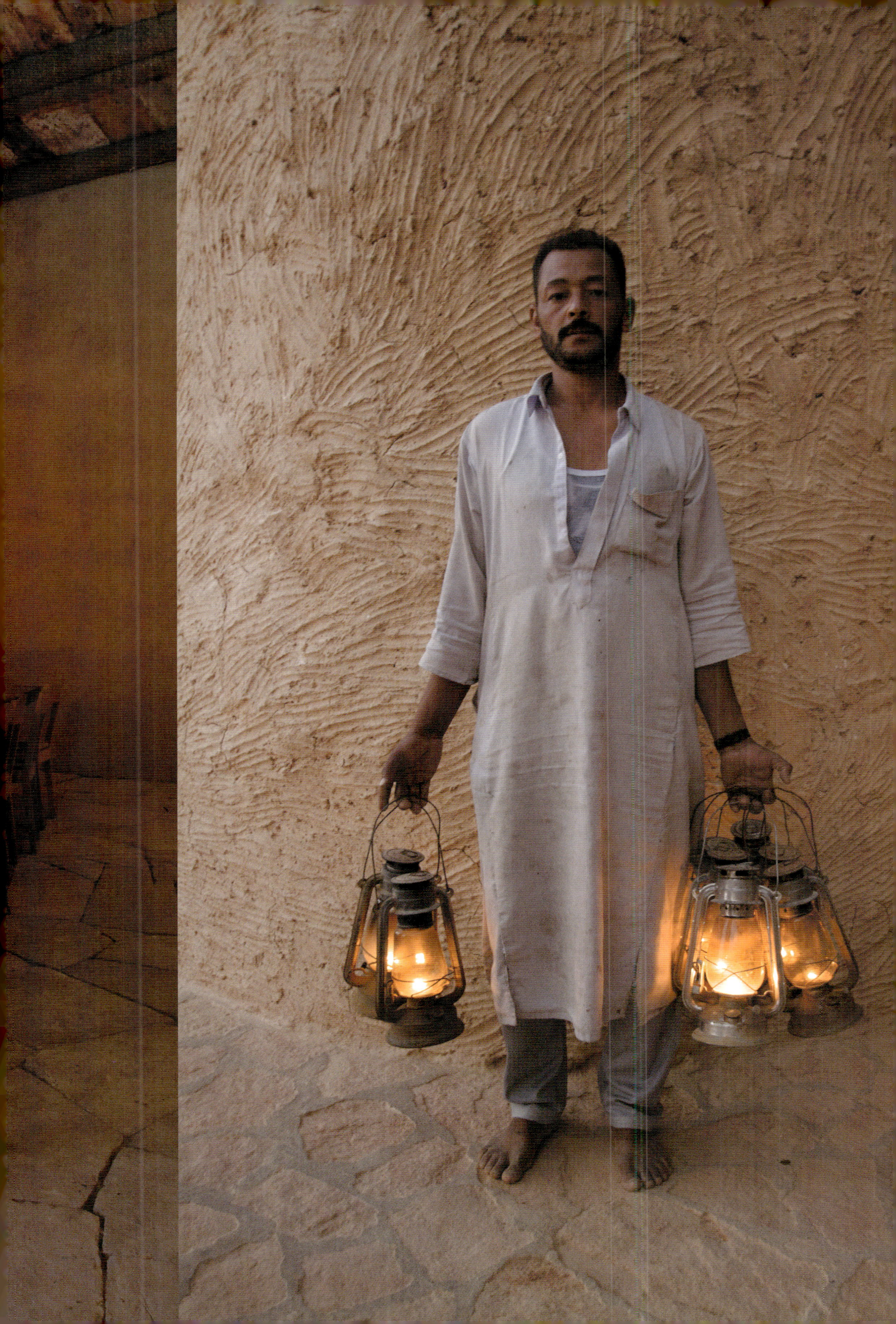

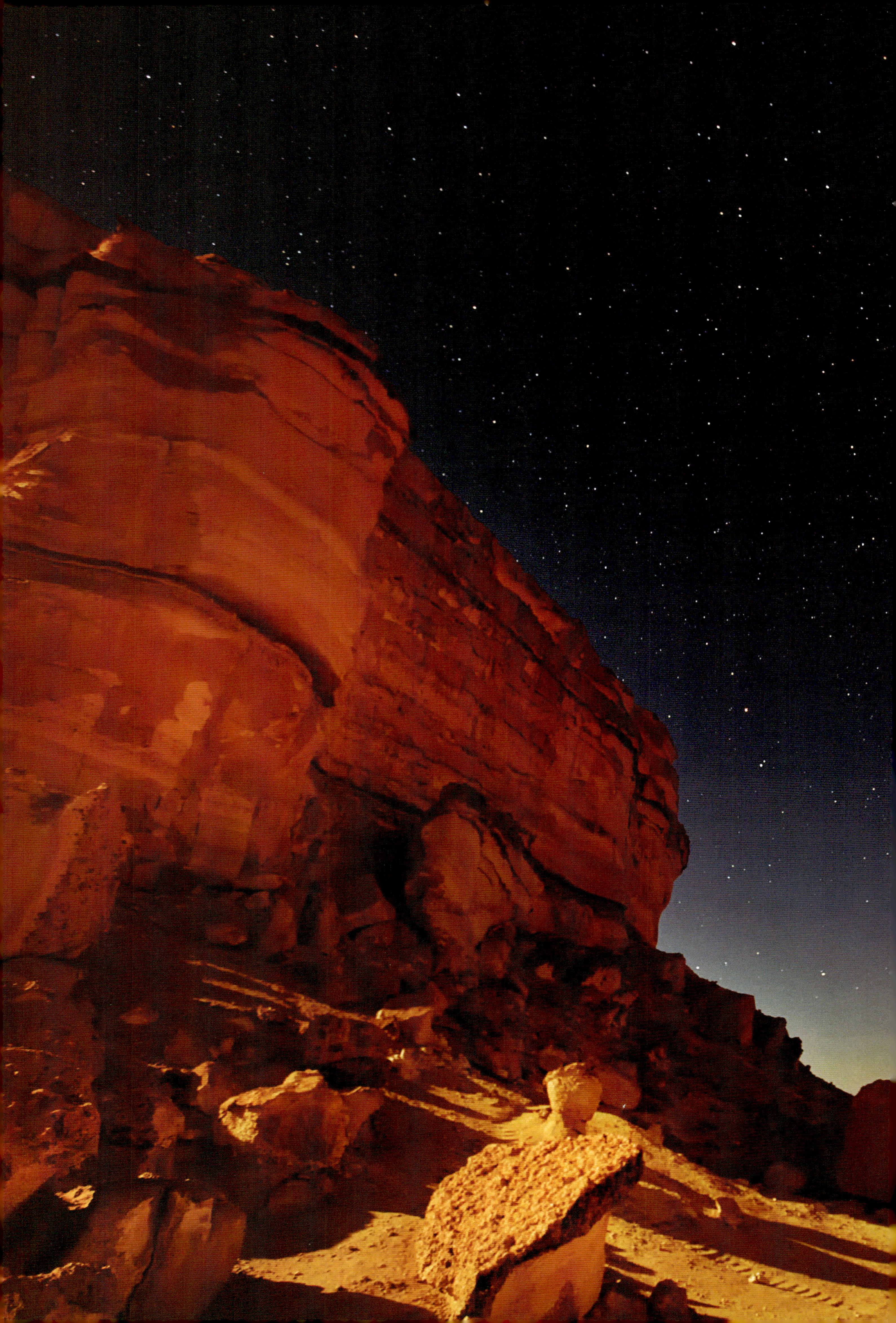

The nighttime sky in Siwa is a flickering wonderland of stars, rarely seen by city dwellers

Dr Mounir Neamatalla hosts dinner at the ecolodge beneath rope-bound beams
Khaled's infectious smile (right) welcomes guests as he serves up strong Arabic coffee

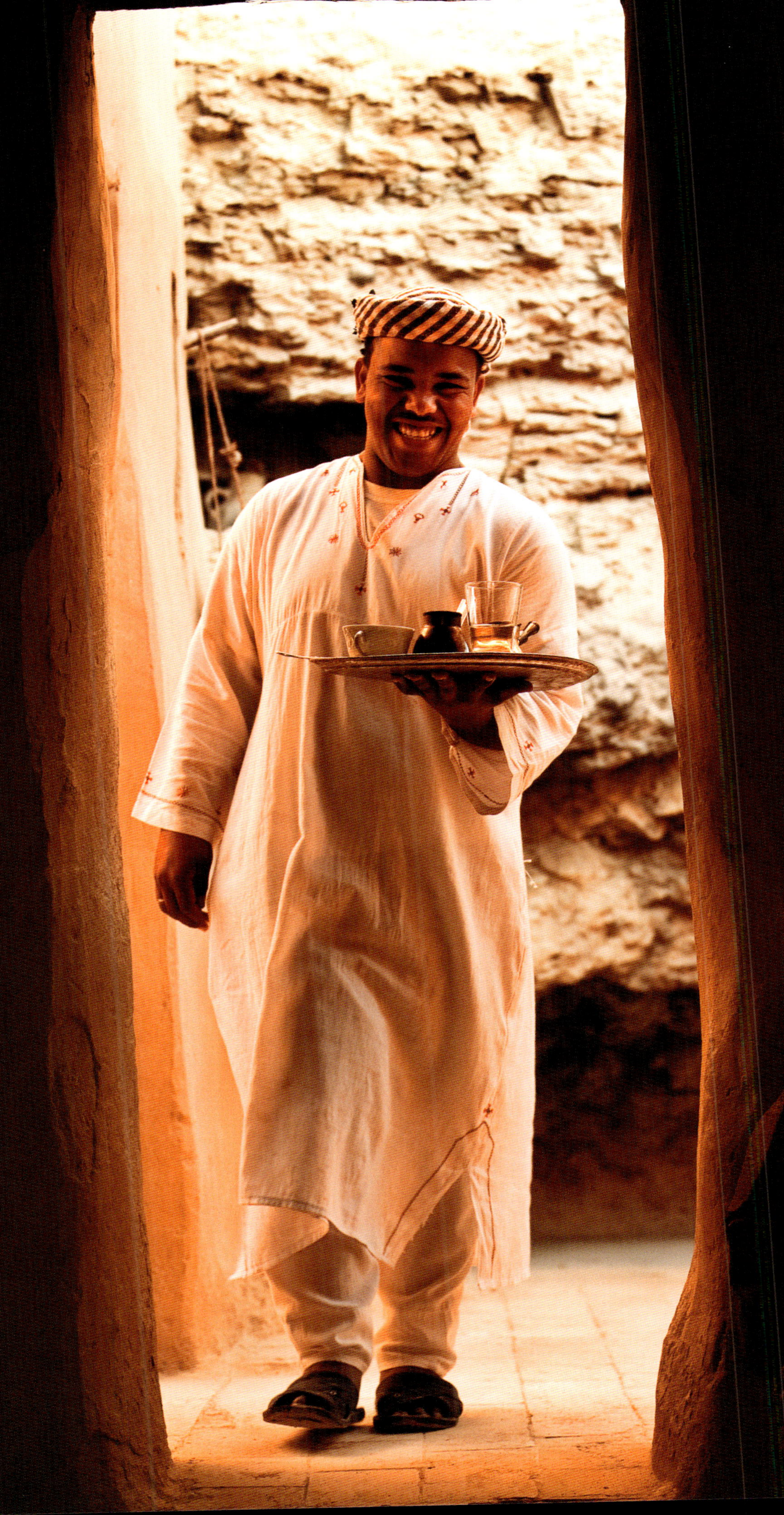

Abdul Hayy L. Holdij'
Associate Chair, American University in C

SILENCE. WHAT IS SILENCE? IN MY LIFE, I HAVE EXPERIENCED THE SILENCE OF ASHRAMS AND ZENDOS, OF SEAS AND MOUNTAINS, OF THE NIGHT AND CLOSED ROOMS, AND OF CIRCUMAMBULATIONS OF STUPAS AND THE KAABA. EACH KIND HAS A TEXTURE, A TASTE, A STILLNESS. PERHAPS THAT IS A BETTER WORD: STILLNESS.

It is in stillness that emotions rise and fall, perceptions are clarified, priorities are reconsidered and the mind is settled. The stillness of Siwa is ancient, the stillness of desert.

A place where desert, water and sky meet in perfect symbiosis; where events take place in the timelessness of the elements and are shaped in a dreamscape; where vision and illusion meet seamlessly.

True, there are all the activities of humans that take place, and they produce sound and movement. Yet, they arise, they fall, they focus, they disperse in a vast, still space that has witnessed drifting sands for millennia.

It is an oasis. The Prophet Mohammed, peace and blessings be upon him, says that we are in this world as travelers, moving across the vast limitlessness of existence, only to rest for a while in an oasis, under a palm tree, and then to continue our journey into that vast limitlessness again.

And that is Siwa—a place to still your troubled mind, to place things in perspective, to re-orient and re-charge yourself before continuing your journey.

You may imagine a young conqueror traversing this vast expanse of sand to ask for the purpose of his existence from the oracle at Siwa.

And maybe it was the process of stripping away, of becoming less and less in the presence of an endless vista of sand, of arriving humbled and awed by this lush green jewel set in the dry desert, that prepared him to receive the message of the oracle.

Was it what Alexander learned in Siwa that made him leave instructions that he should be carried with his empty hands showing during his funeral procession, as a sign and a lesson? Stripped down to an ultimate stillness out of which all forms arise and return to?

Siwa itself is the oracle. The place that puts your life, your ambitions, your hopes and fears, into perspective.

You have to traverse that space, breathe in the clarity of the air, open your pores to the quiet, and settle your mind. Then, you will truly experience Siwa.

The Sahara dunes under a blue sky; the horizon appears endless, infinite

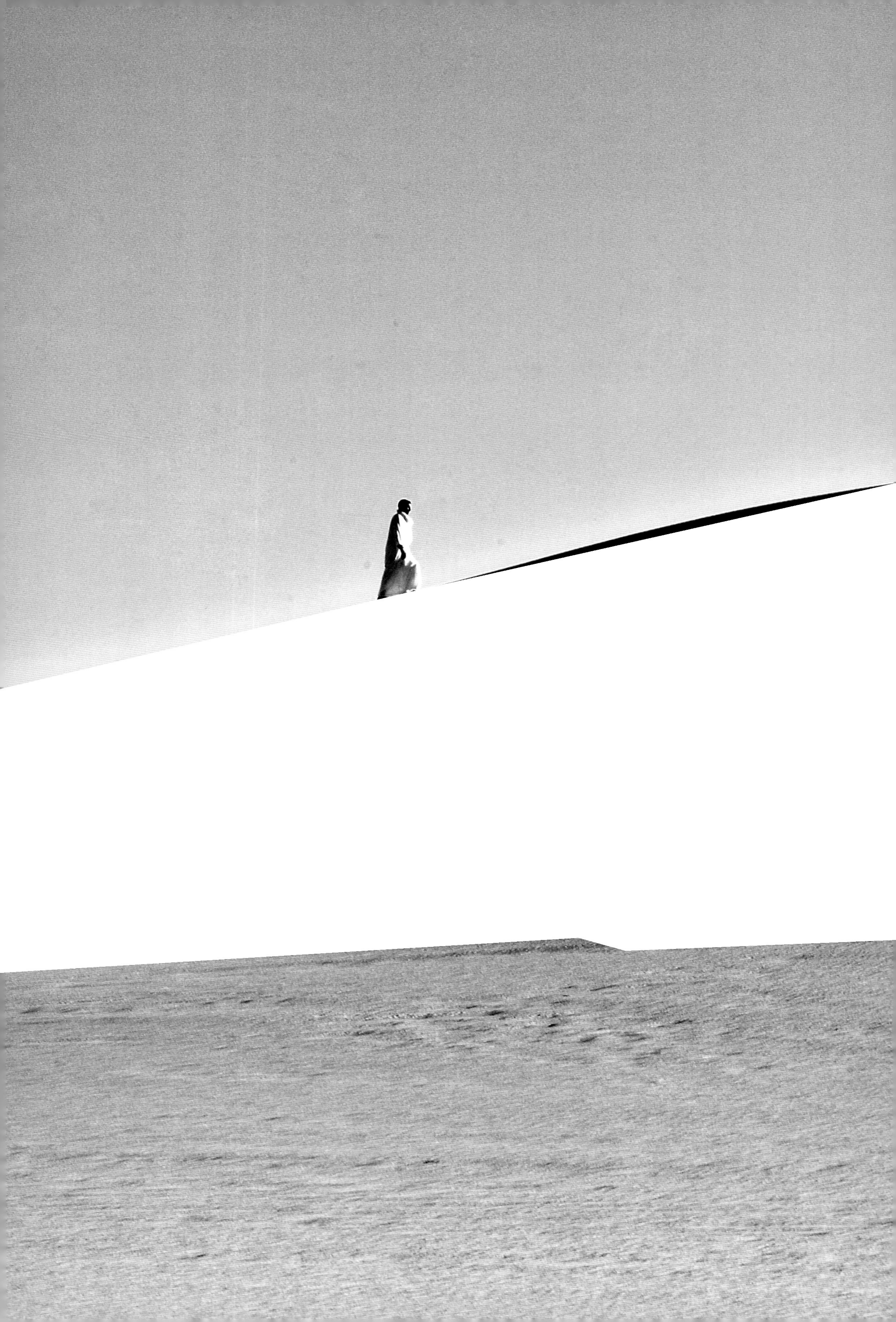

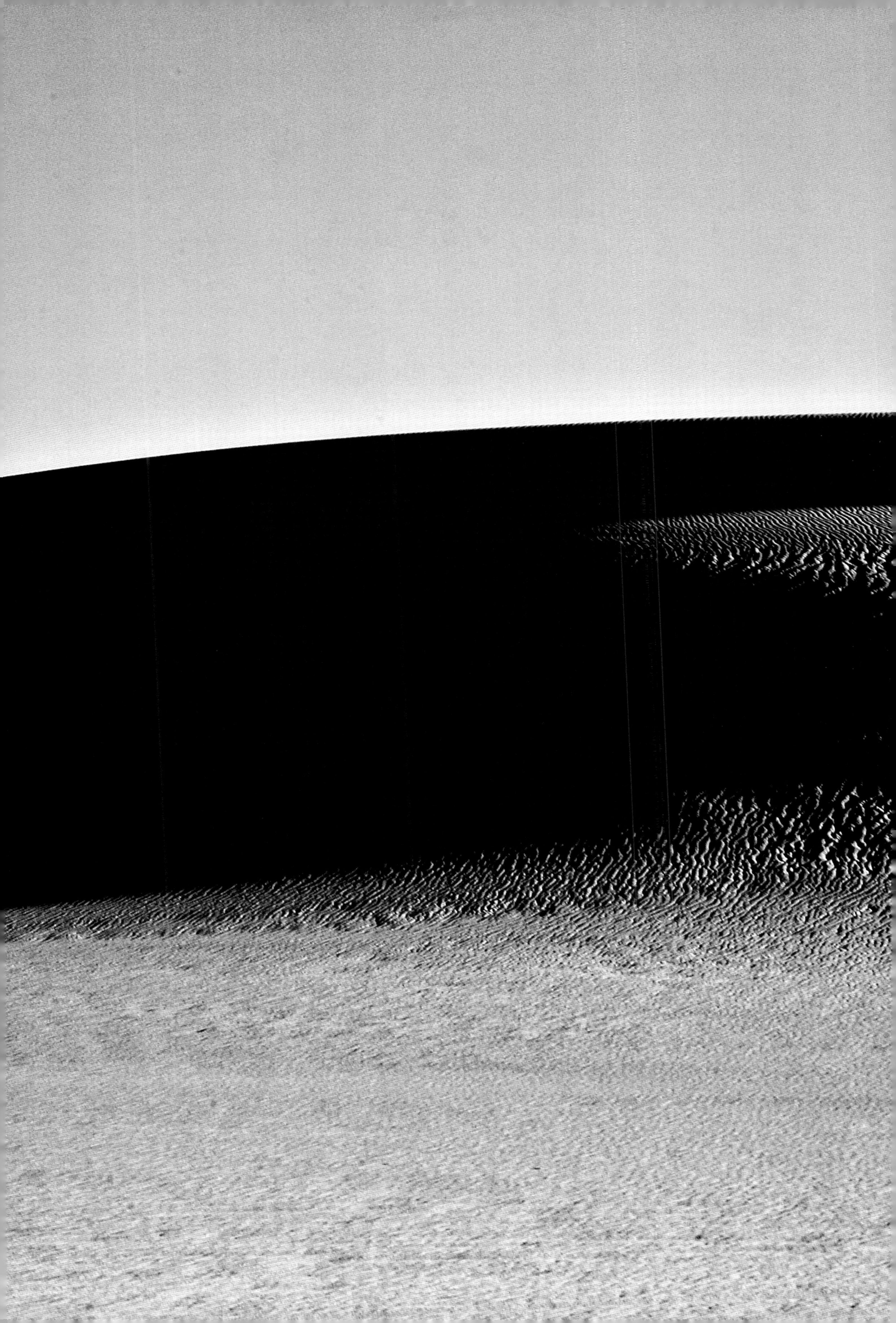

The Siyaha Festival is a study in fraternity: here, men young and old are preparing a feast for the communal village meal

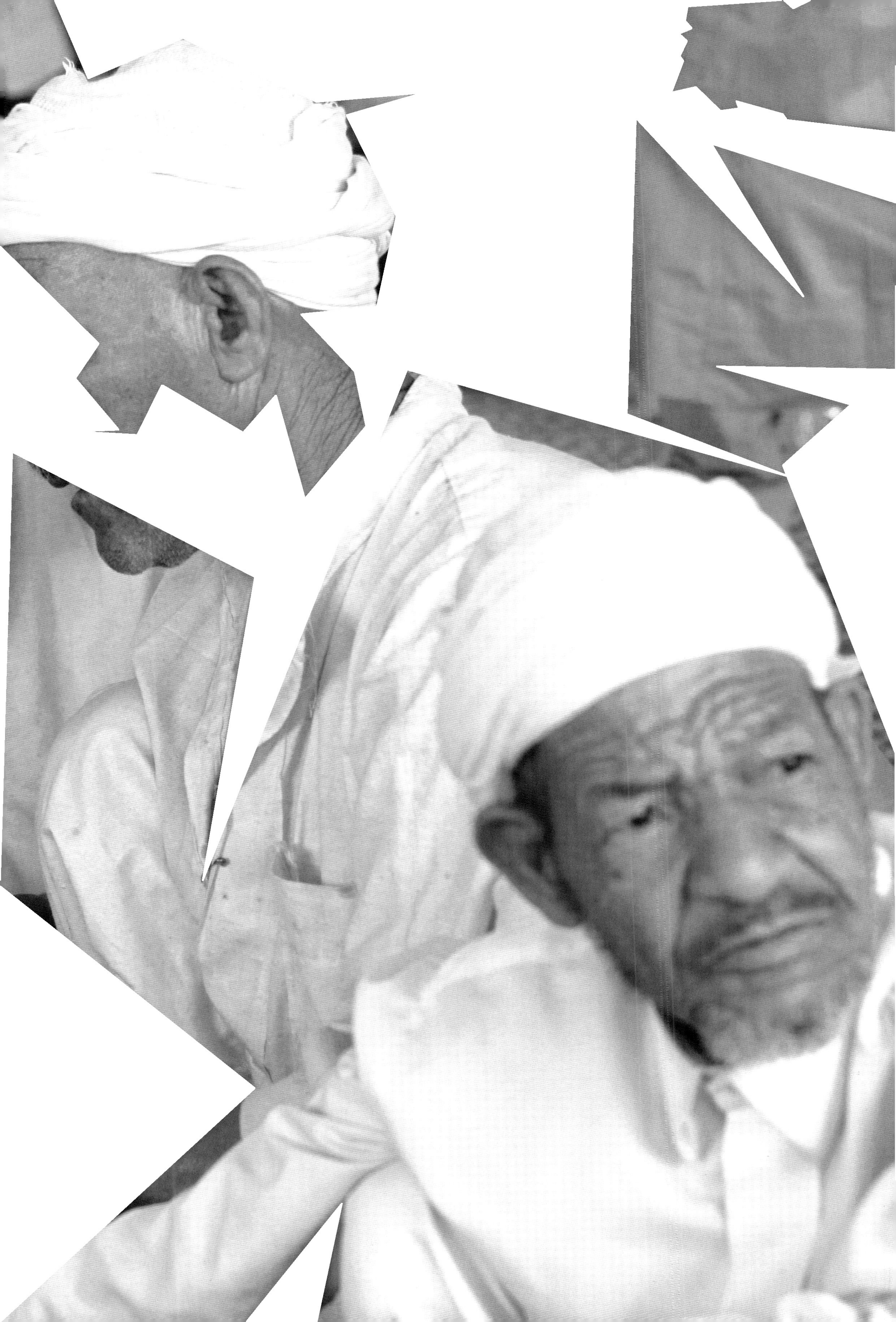

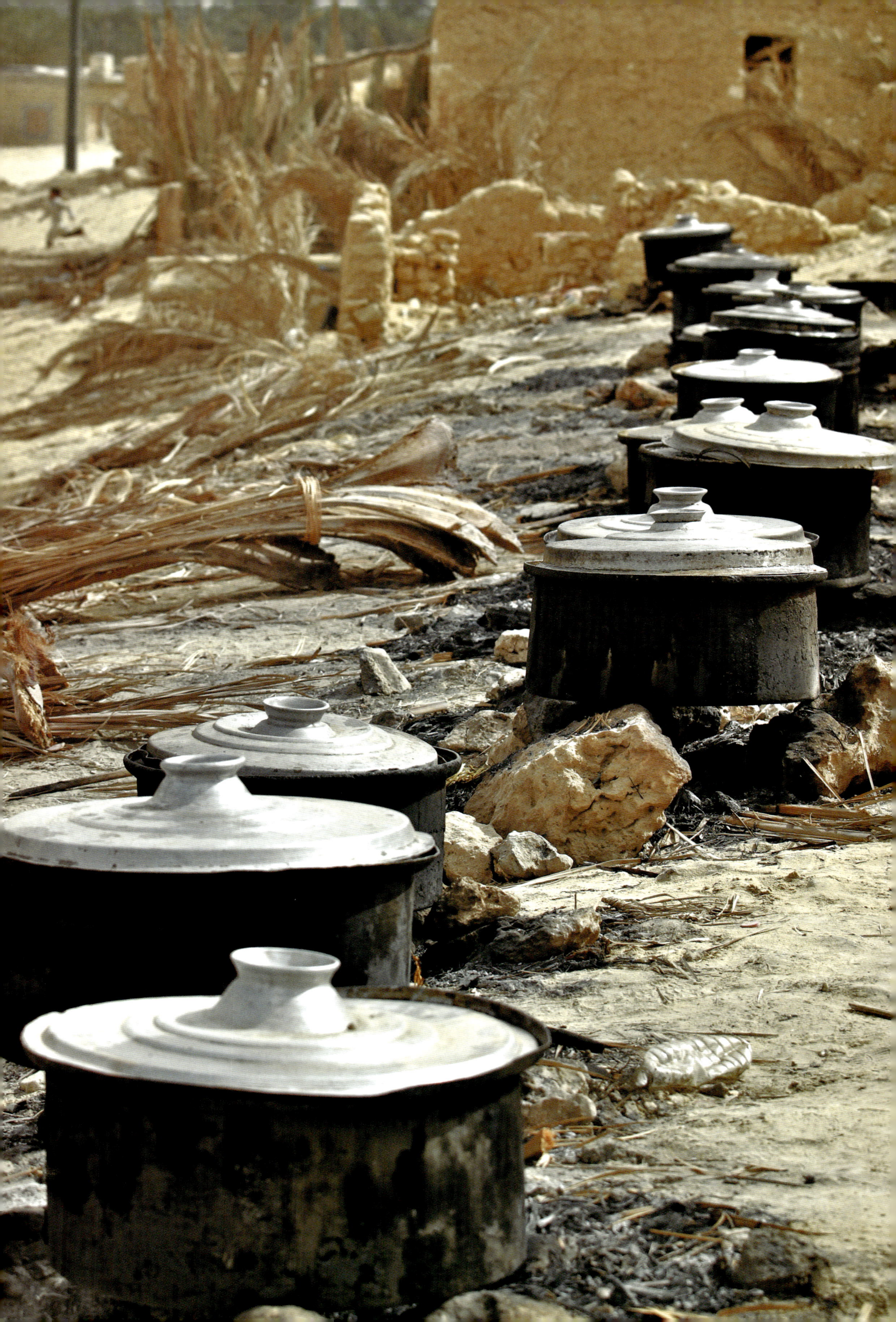

During Siyaha Festival, pots of food are lined up (left) to feed the entire town as a gesture of togetherness

In the evening, a man kneels silently for prayer

Worshippers perform the zikr, a spiritual chant extolling God

The oldest man in Siwa smiles, an expression telling of a life well lived
A young man in the town center (right) runs a sand-dune surfboard rental shop

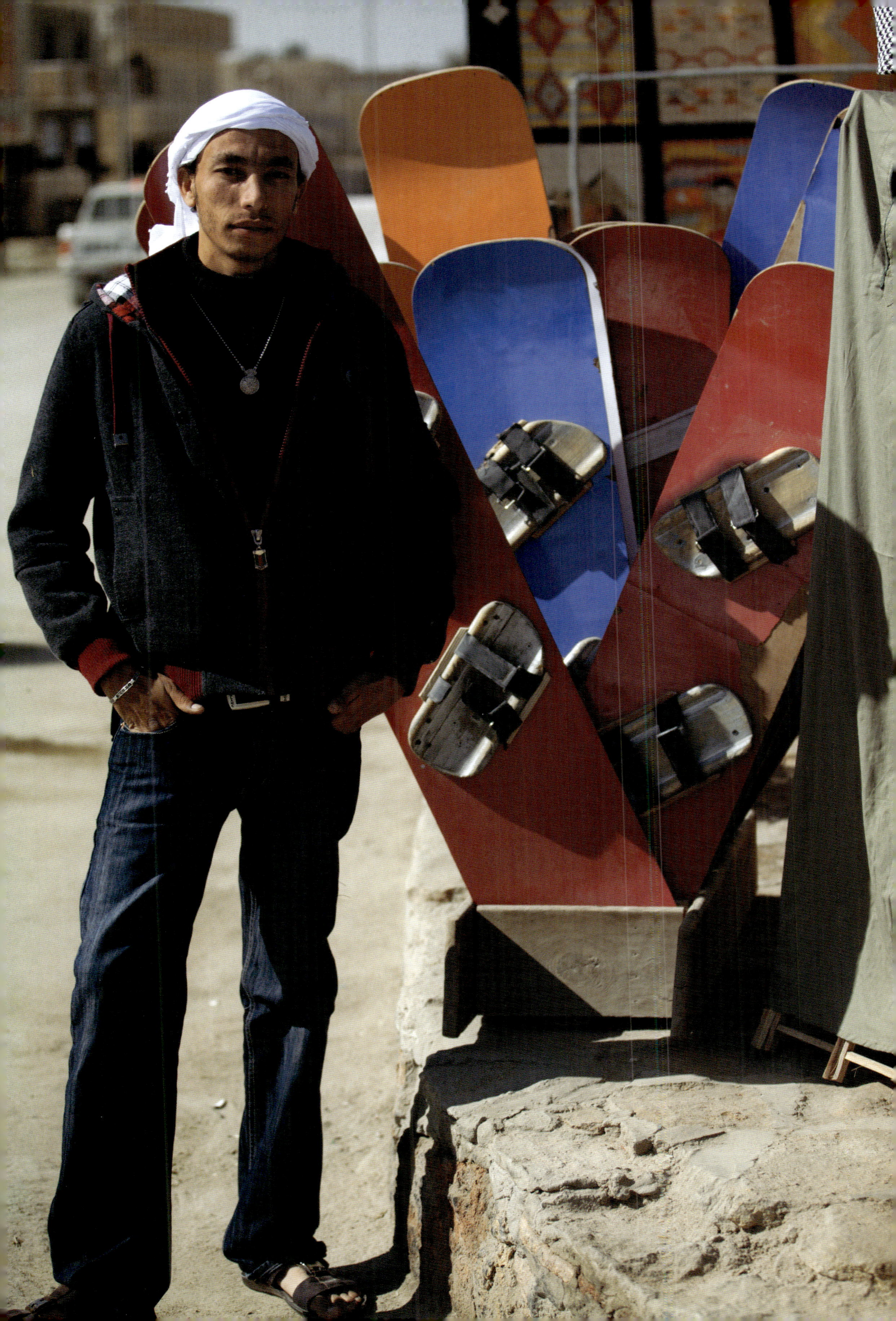

RANA CHALABI
Artist

A **FRIEND OF MINE IS AN AMAZING COMPOSER**. ONCE, SOMEBODY ASKED HIM ABOUT THE SOURCE OF INSPIRATION FOR HIS MUSIC. HIS ANSWER WAS: "I JUST HEAR IT." WELL, ARTISTS ARE THE SAME: THEY JUST SEE IT!

The light in Siwa oasis, the vibrations of color, the limpid texture of water in contrast to the ochres and yellows of the desert, all of that is breathtaking.

After seeing and experiencing this magnificent viewscape, it suddenly seems foolish to assume that I could capture it on canvas. But I am driven, and always hopeful that when I hold my brush in hand, I am able to catch a fleeting moment of that experience: an impression of sky, a reflection on the water, the sound of palms.

I always like to use watercolors in Siwa because of their transparency, the fleeting nature of their application. The use of these materials allows me to reflect some of the serenity, tranquility and joy that the place brings to my soul. In a way, it is my personal meditation and connection to Siwa's beauty.

Painting Siwa allows me to marvel at its creation, but also to be part of it all!

A scene capturing the traditional mud-brick finishes of the Adrere Amellal properties

Rana Chalabi expresses Siwa's breathtaking nature and colors in her watercolor paintings

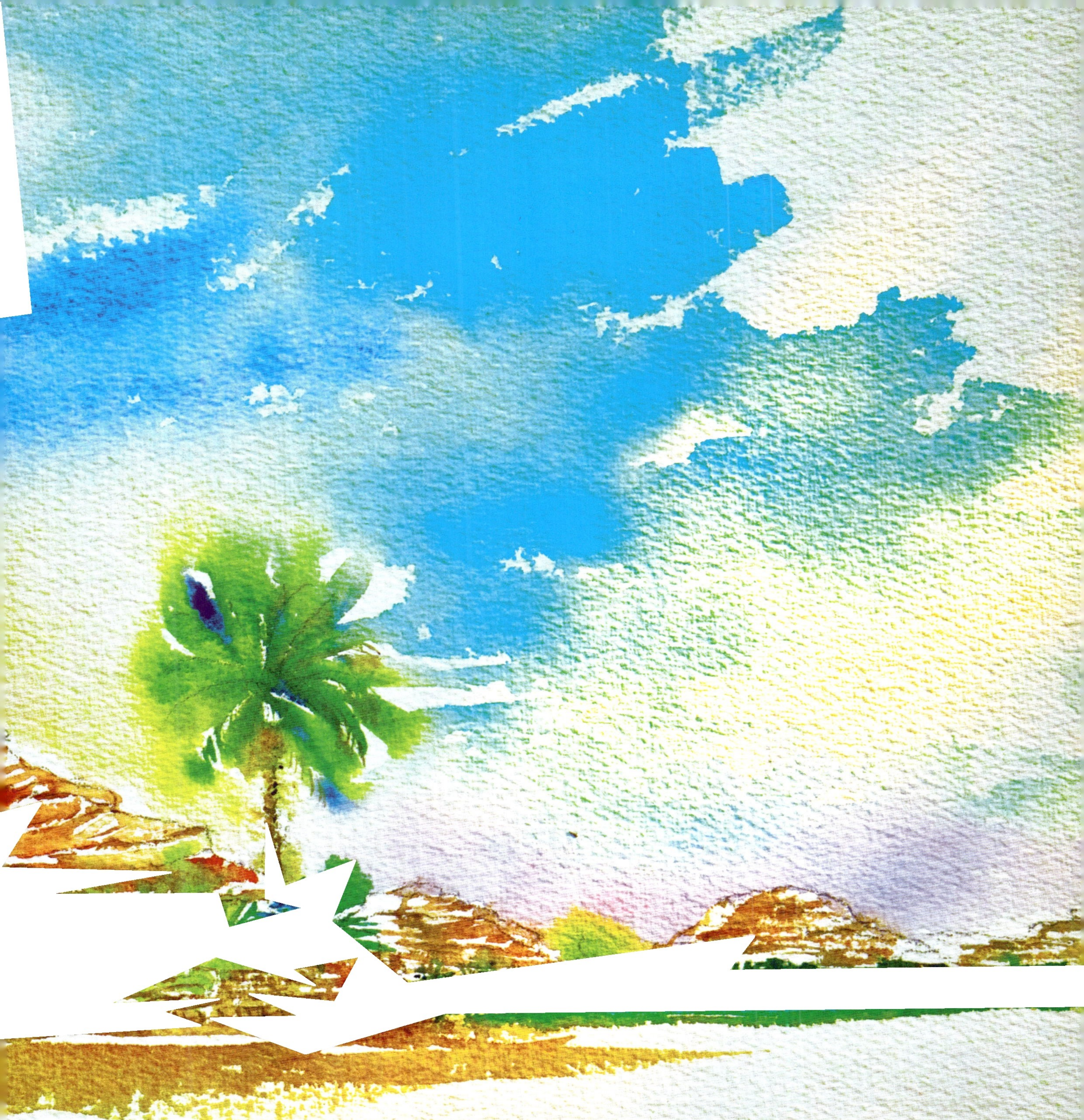

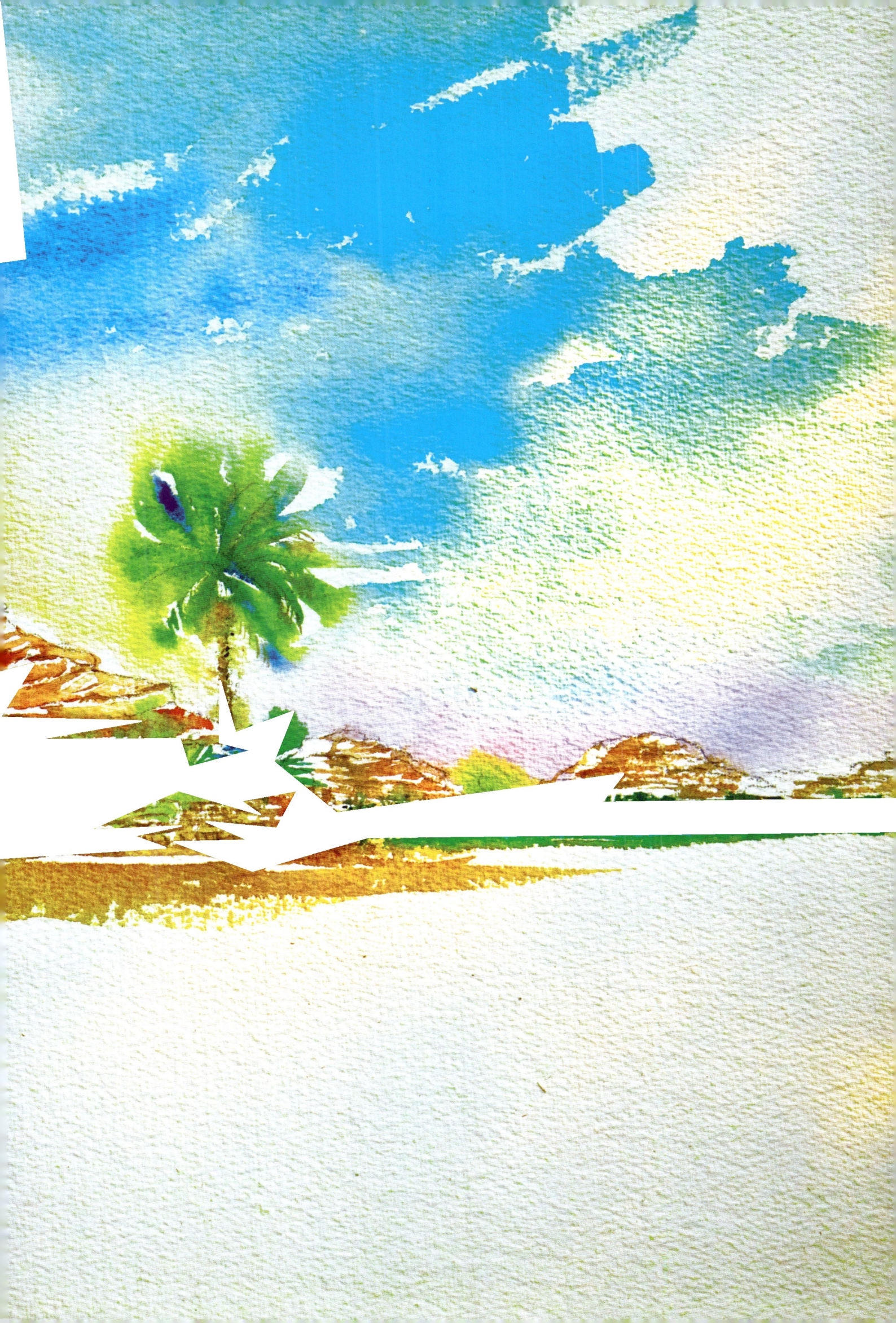

Lanterns and stars show the way at night at Adrere Amellal

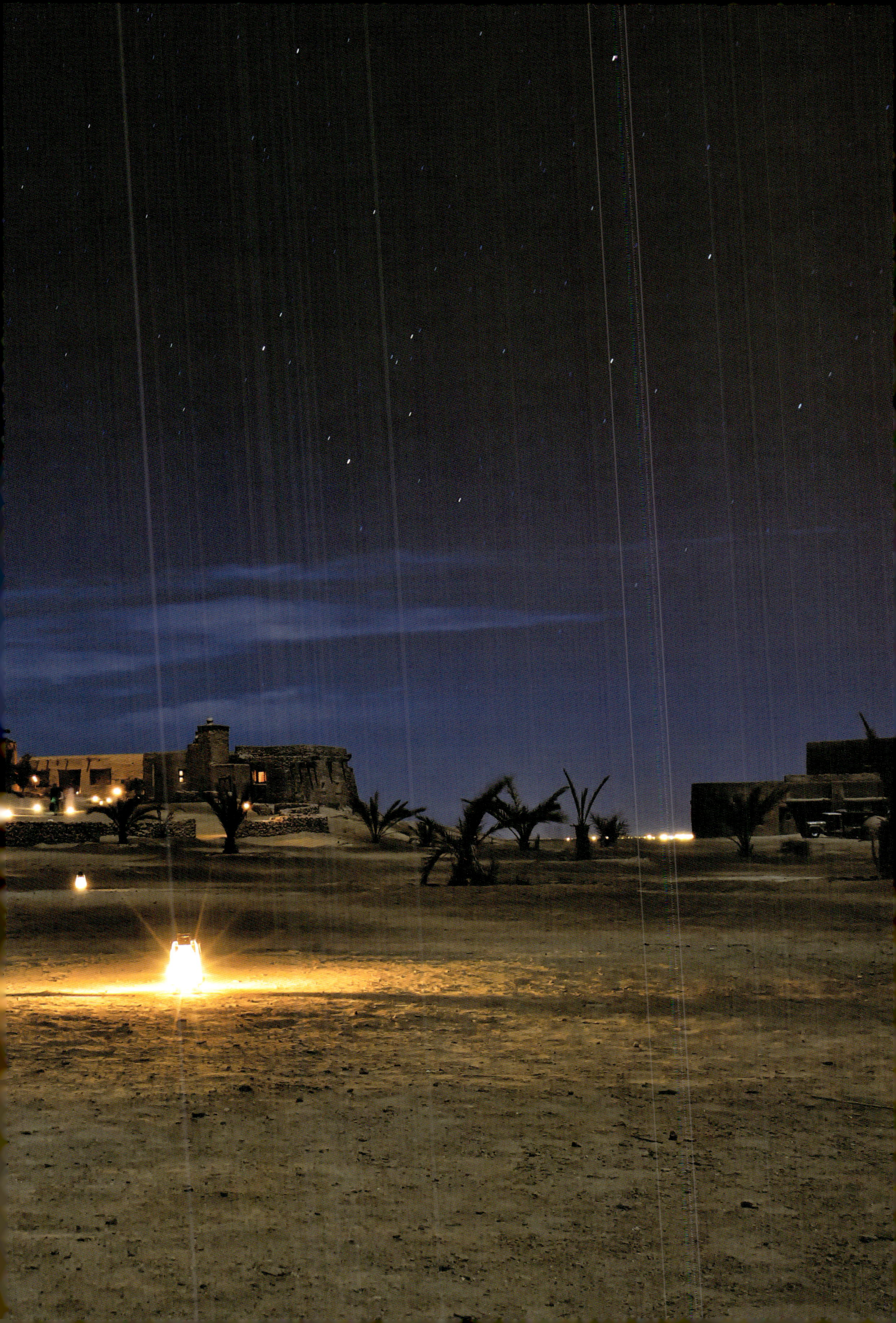

Gazing out at the herb garden and the lake beyond from Tamazid Villa's terrace, the house India Mahdavi designed in Siwa

INDIA MAHDAVI
Architect, designer

IN 1998, I TRAVELED TO EGYPT FOR THE FIRST TIME—LATE, CONSIDERING THAT MY MOTHER IS EGYPTIAN. WHEN I SAW THE NILE, I WAS MOVED TO TEARS. PERHAPS IT WAS THE IMMEDIATE CONNECTION I FELT, OR THE SENSE OF HERITAGE THAT WAS LONG IN COMING: THERE WAS A FEELING OF HAVING ARRIVED HOME.

I continued on to Siwa with Dr Mounir Neamatalla and my family. After the long drive, to be greeted by open fires, candlelight and that lunar atmosphere was like a vision out of a dream. That was the first time I actually acknowledged being part of this planet; it was as if it was introducing itself to me for the first time, its open skies, earth and galaxies in full display and intimately close. The White Mountain seemed to cradle us underneath it; it was so majestic and nurturing—like nature's own deity.

I am a builder by nature, it's what I do, so it didn't take long for me to get involved with Dr Mounir's architectural work for the ecolodge, Adrere Amellal. I admired the way he took great care in fine-tuning the builders' work section by section until he had the structure he wanted. It unfolded organically, finally looking as if it were an extension of the mountain itself. We had constant conversations about structure, function, flow and design. Siwa became my muse, inspiring me to design new products indigenous to its environment, yet updated in function and form. The large assignment eventually came: a standalone villa of about 800m^2 for Dr Mounir, called Tamazid. I wanted a different concept to the vernacular style of the 'ecolodge'. There was a rock in the middle of the site that I treated as a foundation to the building. From there I designed a simple rectangular villa surrounded by the trees and green. We focused on open circulation, high ceilings and capturing views from all windows and terraces. I avoided the small, low-ceilinged niches typical to certain parts of the ecolodge, because I felt for a residence in the desert this was a fantastic opportunity to enjoy scale, volumes and views extravagantly.

We built a beautiful villa in Siwa together and I took up a floor as my personal apartment. Having a home in Siwa meant committing myself to regular visits and getting to know the town and its people. I was particularly intrigued by the different ways of working with salt to produce items of décor and function. I spent time with Salt Master Sayed in his workshop and after several experiments I developed the chunky translucent salt votive that is now a big business in Siwa. In 2009, hundreds were shipped to Art Basel Miami to light up the 1111 parking space designed by Herzog et de Meuron. It was rewarding to see a simple idea developed in a small workshop in the Sahara turn into a product propelling the Siwan economy and attracting important art and design communities abroad.

Later, I turned to working with local craftsmen and women on a variety of products from rope to stone to textiles. With local craftsman Ahmed Ali, we developed interesting uses for rope, such as rope headboards that are both beautiful and robust. I always carry around a book of carbon papers that I use to sketch various designs; I'd give the craftsmen one copy and keep one for myself. We always look forward to this collaboration and it has instilled in them a love for design and creating, so much so that their own work eventually takes a life of its own. They amaze me with their talent. This is the 'human' experience I am fortunate enough to enjoy in Siwa and one that means so much to me, despite the language barrier!

I come back to Siwa twice a year, but I wish I could spend half my time here. Siwa is good for me because it is an open-plan laboratory of ideas, prototypes, resources and concepts. It feeds me creatively while its positive spiritual energy and glorious nature give me balance. With Siwa it's different, because it always promises to give back whatever I put in, multiple times over. I couldn't ask for more, both as a designer and as a person.

Siwa's passionate advocate, Dr Mounir Neamatalla, on the terrace of Tamazid Villa, where he is often found (above)

The villa's pools were designed to mimic Siwa's famous natural springs dating back to antiquity, and exalted by Herodotus in the 5th century BC (below)

Friends (opposite) lounge in one of the villa's many relaxing entertaining spaces

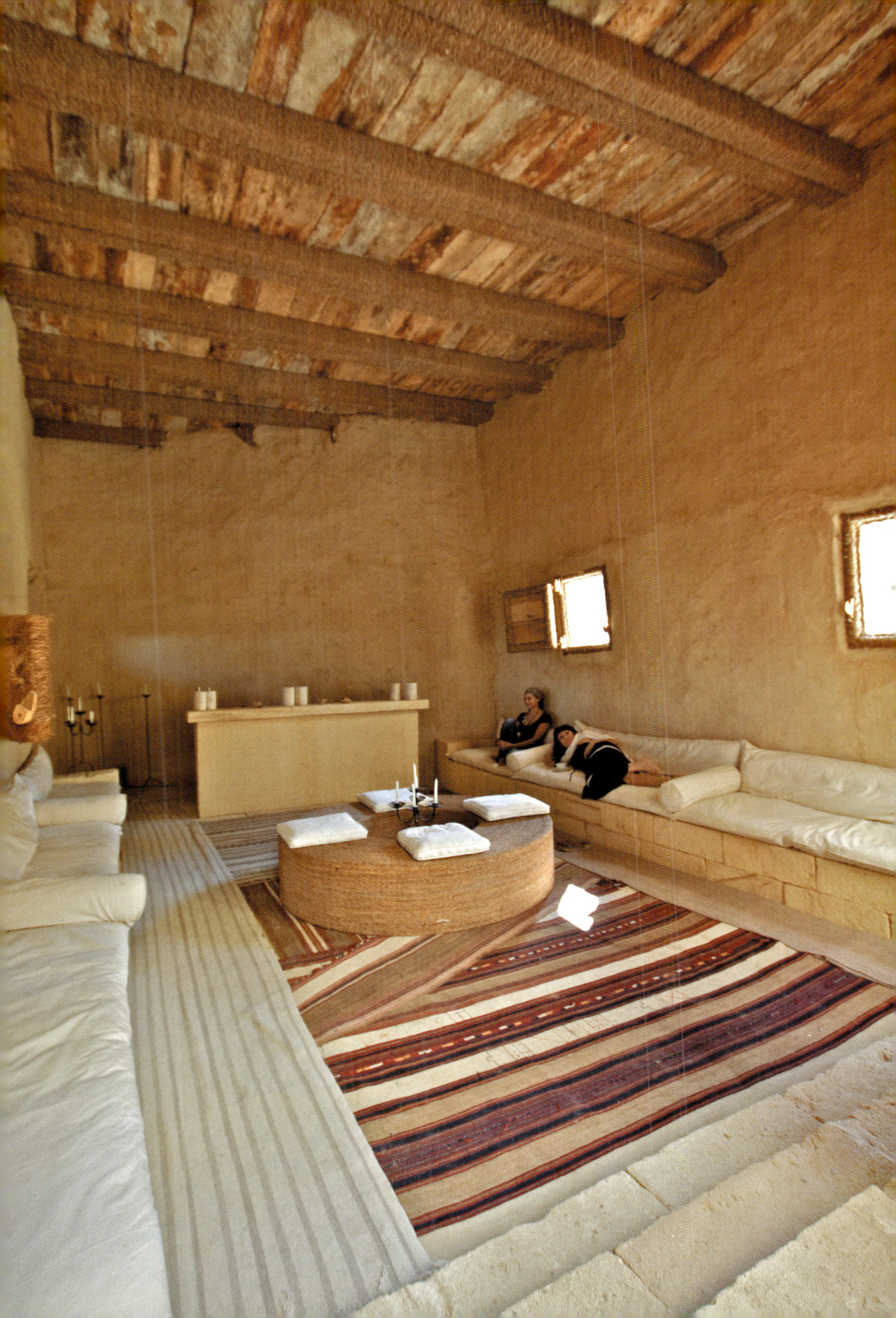

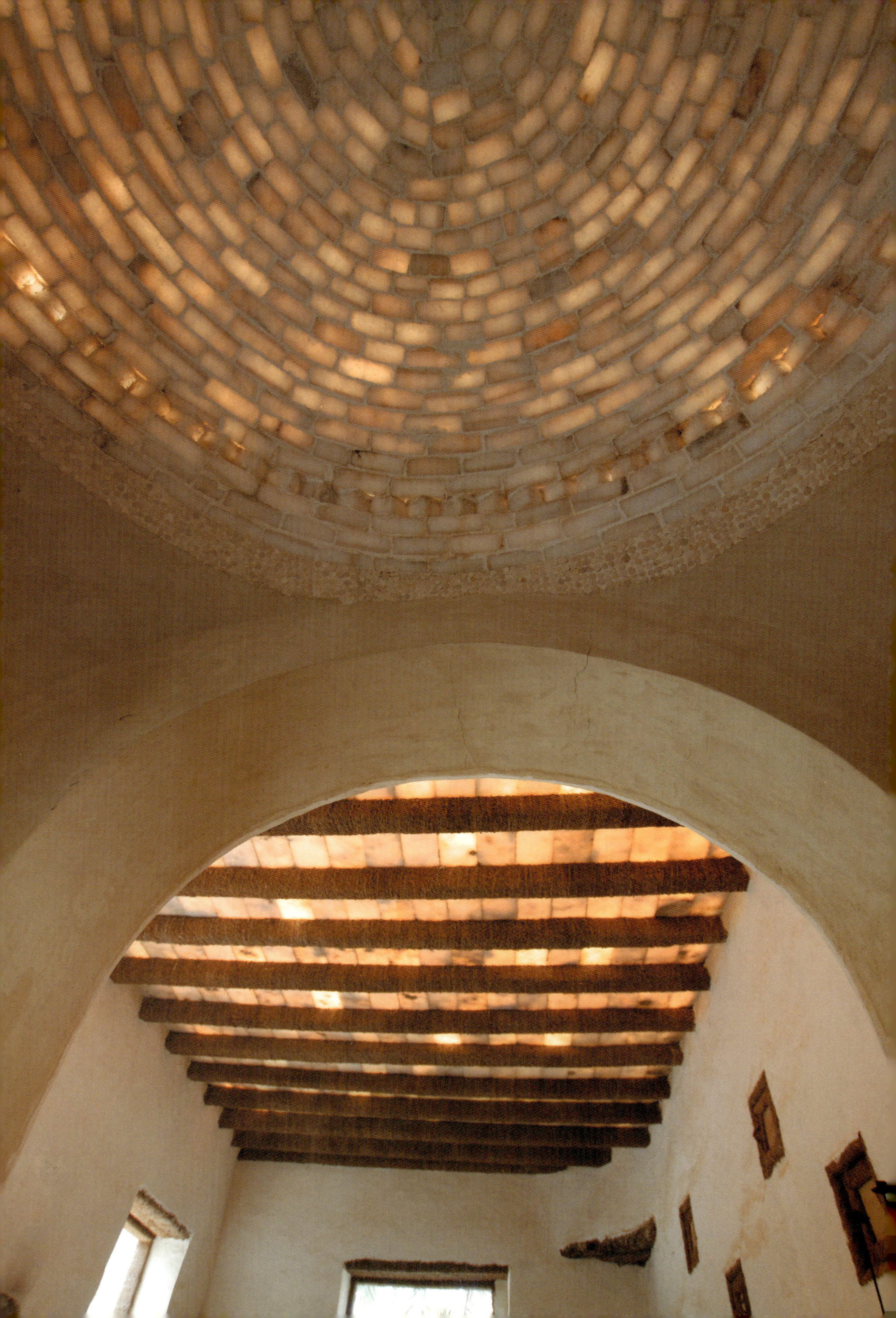

Ceilings (opposite) are tiled with Siwa's most abundant resource, salt, which casts a mysterious, romantic glow in the evenings

Tamazid is built using the ancient technique of Kershef, reinterpreted thoughtfully for modern living

A daybed on the roof has 360° degree views of stunning oasis nature

Fresh after a winter rainstorm, the earth, sky and vegetation around Tamazid take on a spectacular depth

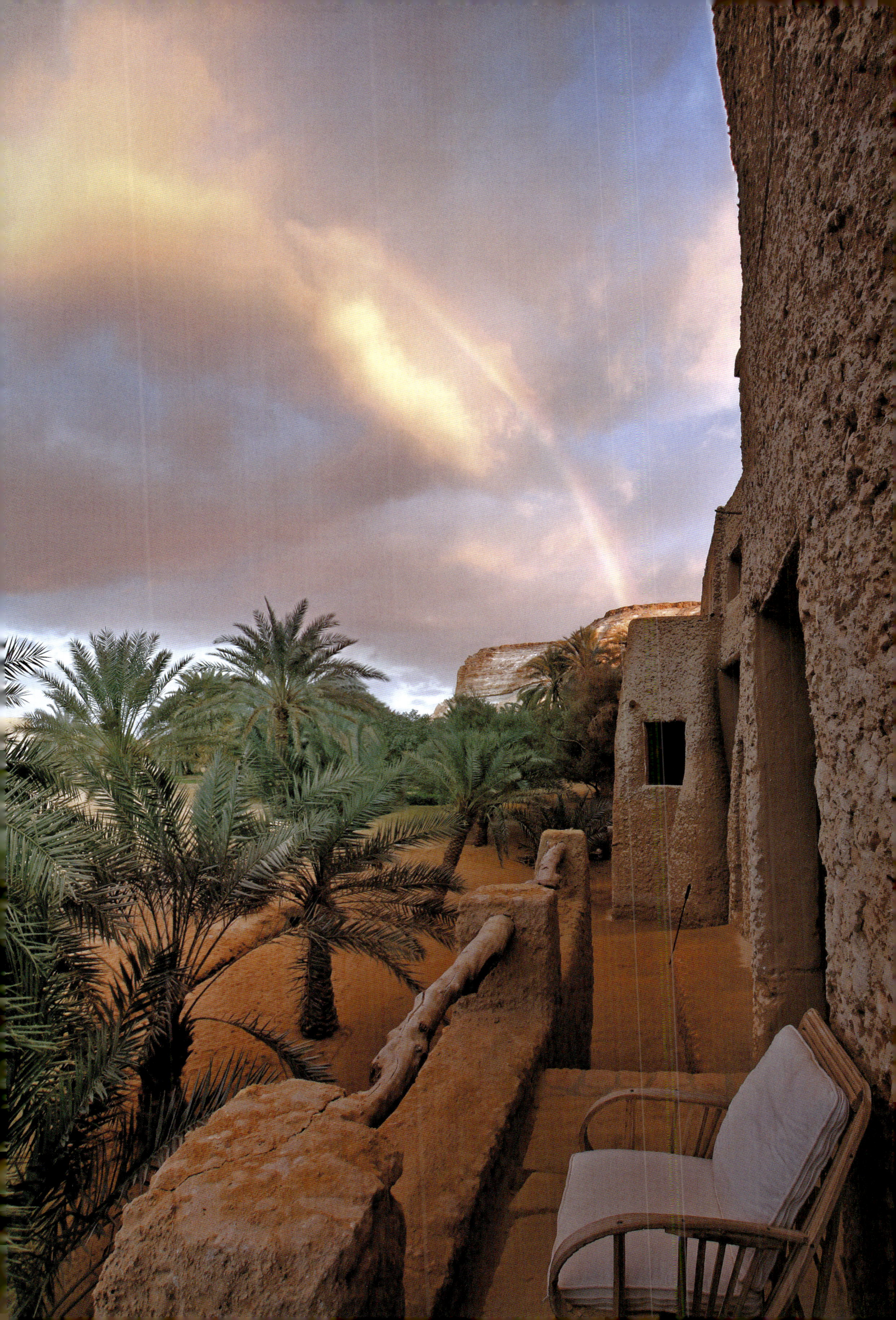

SAYED ABOUL KASEM
Salt Master

I STARTED WORKING WITH SALT AROUND 13 YEARS AGO, UNDER THE TUTELAGE OF DR MOUNIR. BEFORE THEN, NO ONE IN SIWA HAD THOUGHT OF USING THE SALT ABUNDANT IN ITS LAKES FOR ANYTHING OTHER THAN SEASONING FOOD.

We developed and produced the salt tiles that clad some of the walls at Tamazid and the ecolodge. Years later, I had the good fortune of working with India Mahdavi, who came up with the idea of the salt votives. That inspired me to design and develop table lamps, expanding the product line to include hanging ceiling lights as well. They are beautiful when lit; I never tire of admiring them. My work supplies the ecolodge and its sister properties exclusively, but I was very pleased when two of our salt stools were shipped to France! Who would have imagined it? We had produced the stools out of salt for the pianists performing at the music festival at Siwa.

Our largest item is our salt bed. We make the entire headboard and base out of salt in large blocks, along with bedside tables, and they can be seen in some of the bedrooms at the ecolodge and villas.

Working with salt is time consuming. It requires cutting and carving with heavy machinery, followed by careful finishing work by hand. I do love it, though, and when I walk through the town center on my way to the workshop, I see copycat versions of our salt votives and other items being sold in the souk. I look at them quickly and walk on; the quality is a disaster.

otives produced by Salt Master Sayed (above & below); hundreds were shipped to Art Basel Miami in 2009

Salt-brick ceiling at Tamazid (above)
Room divider made from hanging salt spheres (below)

In Siwa, salt literally comes out of the earth

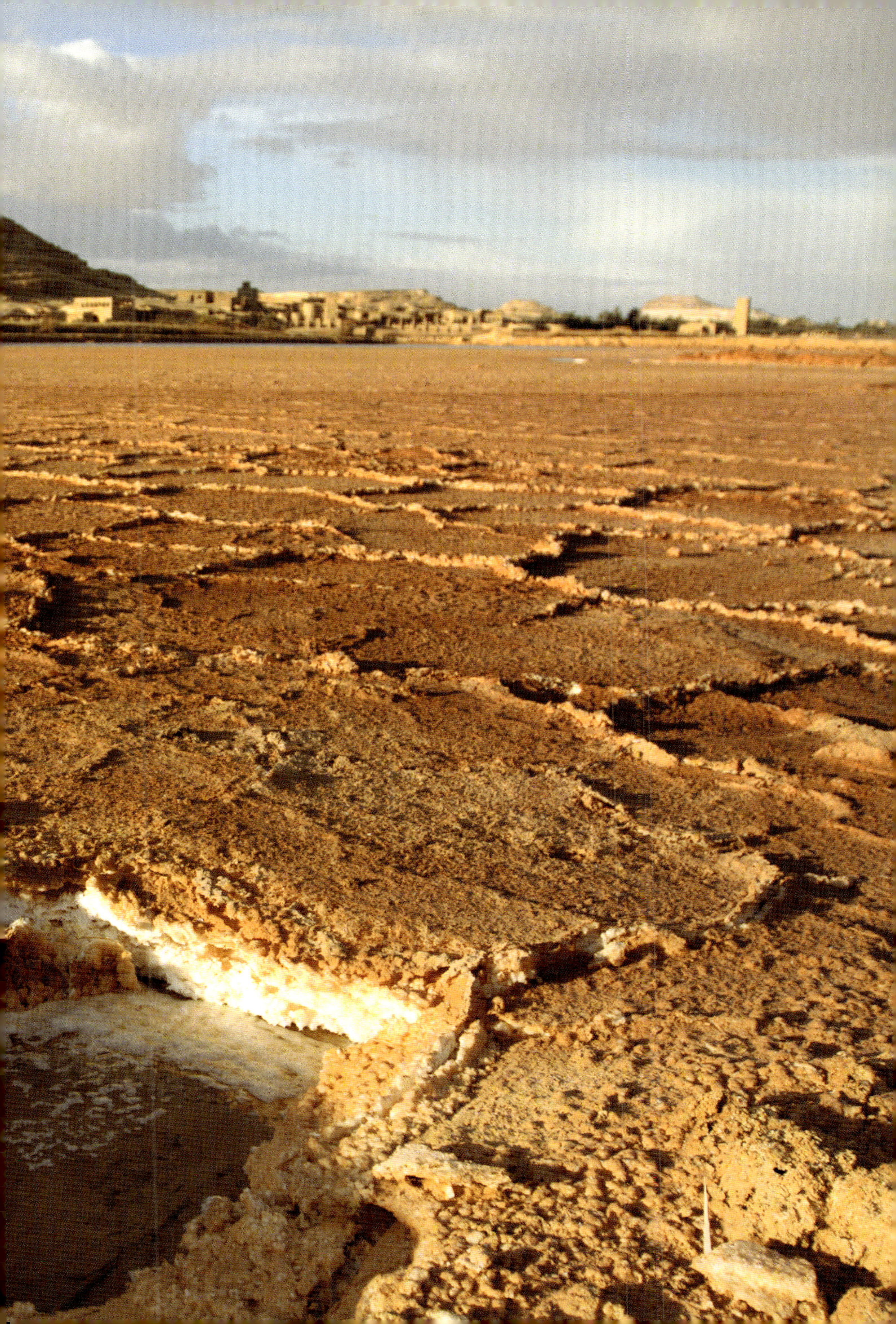

SIWA, SIWA, SIWA YA SIWA ... THIS IS THE CHANT IN MY HEAD WHENEVER I FEEL NOSTALGIC FOR THE BEAUTIFUL SIWA OASIS.

Music and silence combine strongly because music is created within silence and silence is full of music. Whenever I play alone, I find I am never alone. The sound of the drum is different here; it is all consuming and inclusive. We can easily reach exaltation without much effort, just by letting go of what we know as 'normal' or 'everyday' sounds, absorbing instead the core rhythm and chant of the music.

Repetitive, deliberate, constant, but most of all passionate; it transcends time and place, lifting us so that it feels like we are hovering slightly above the earth. This is how music feels in Siwa. When I learned more about the place, I discovered that within the traditions of its Sufi roots, men recreate this rhythmic exaltation with their voices on Mount Dakrour during the Siyaha festival, performing the *zikr*. With repetitive regular chanting that evokes the qualities of the higher being, they go on and on until they are swept away by the moment, levitating spiritually, but always together with hands firmly clasped, in fraternal bondage.

Playing in Siwa brings out a lot of emotions, not only in the musicians themselves, but also in those bearing witness. The nature of the rhythm transports, filling space and silence completely, and uniting everyone present. It is the same in the *zikr;* onlookers may at first feel detached or even skeptical, but as the rhythm rises in its haunting way, they inadvertently become part of the experience, captivated by the hypnotic pull of the beat.

In Siwa music, spirituality and nature are strongly connected. And that is why, as a musician, and especially as a tabla player, I am very moved here, probably more than any other place in the world. However, to the people of Siwa I am an outsider. Moreover, I am a woman in a town where women are hidden away and music is a man's world. It is a challenge because women are not allowed to participate in musical gatherings. It took time and many visits for them to allow me into their space, to play alongside them as an equal. I had to earn their respect before the art of collaborative creation could begin.

Siwan music is made up of tribal transic rhythms, in the Berber tradition. It is simple, constant, yet powerful. The repetition of the basic tribal beats together with the strength of their chanting creates an atmosphere of delightful celebration. Vocalists sing in Siwi, and without speaking the language it is clear that the core of their song remains within traditional and community contexts. Dancing to the tribal beats is natural, calling on our most primeval instincts to express ourselves through movement.

After many visits to Siwa, I felt I had at long last reached the hearts of some of my fellow musicians. Having realized that connection, we shared a feeling that went beyond the confines of their tribal culture. My identity as a woman from the big city was suddenly unimportant. We were no longer different, as long as we were together in that moment, in the center of that impossible rhythm.

SABRINE
EL HOSSAMY
Tabla player, recording artist

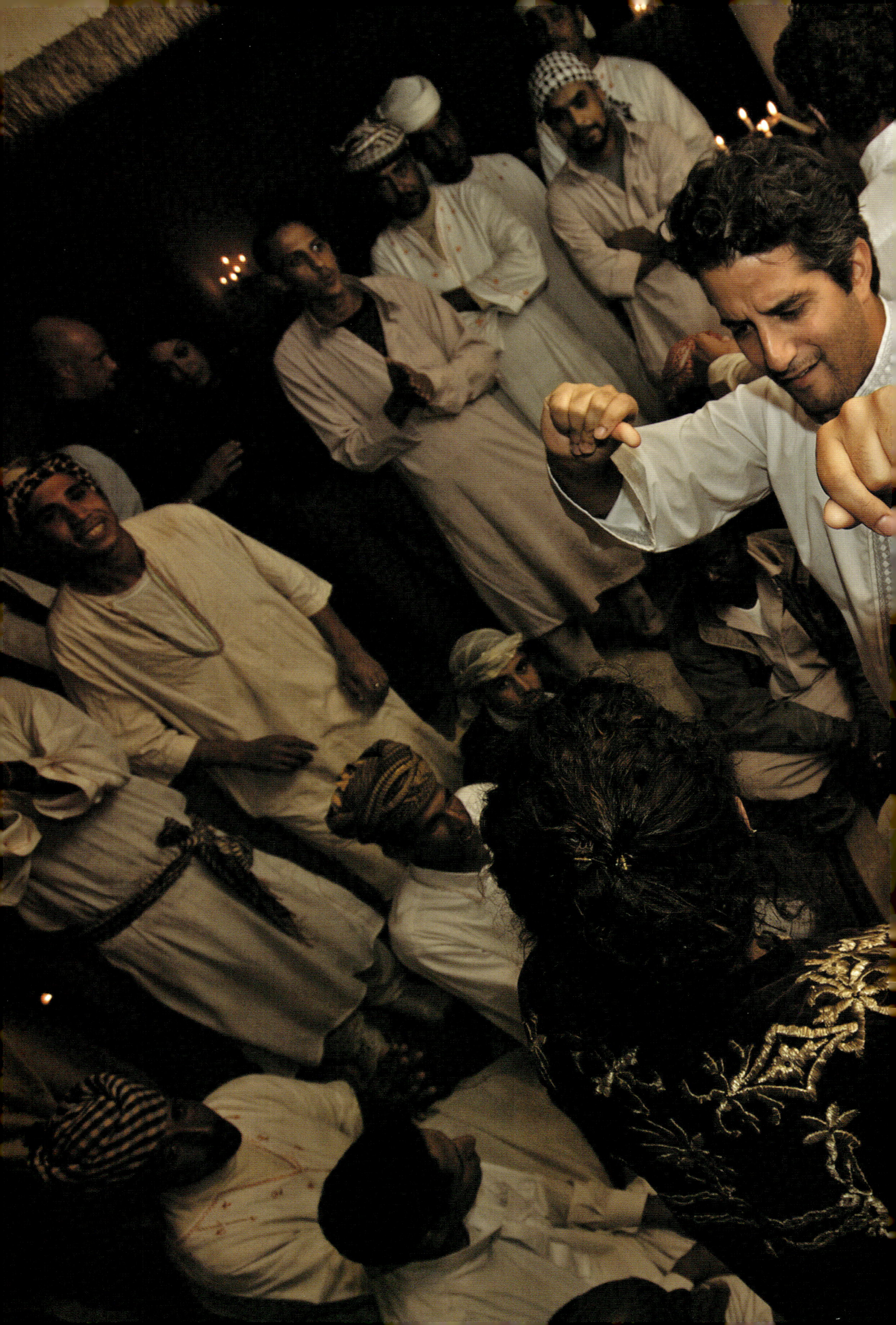

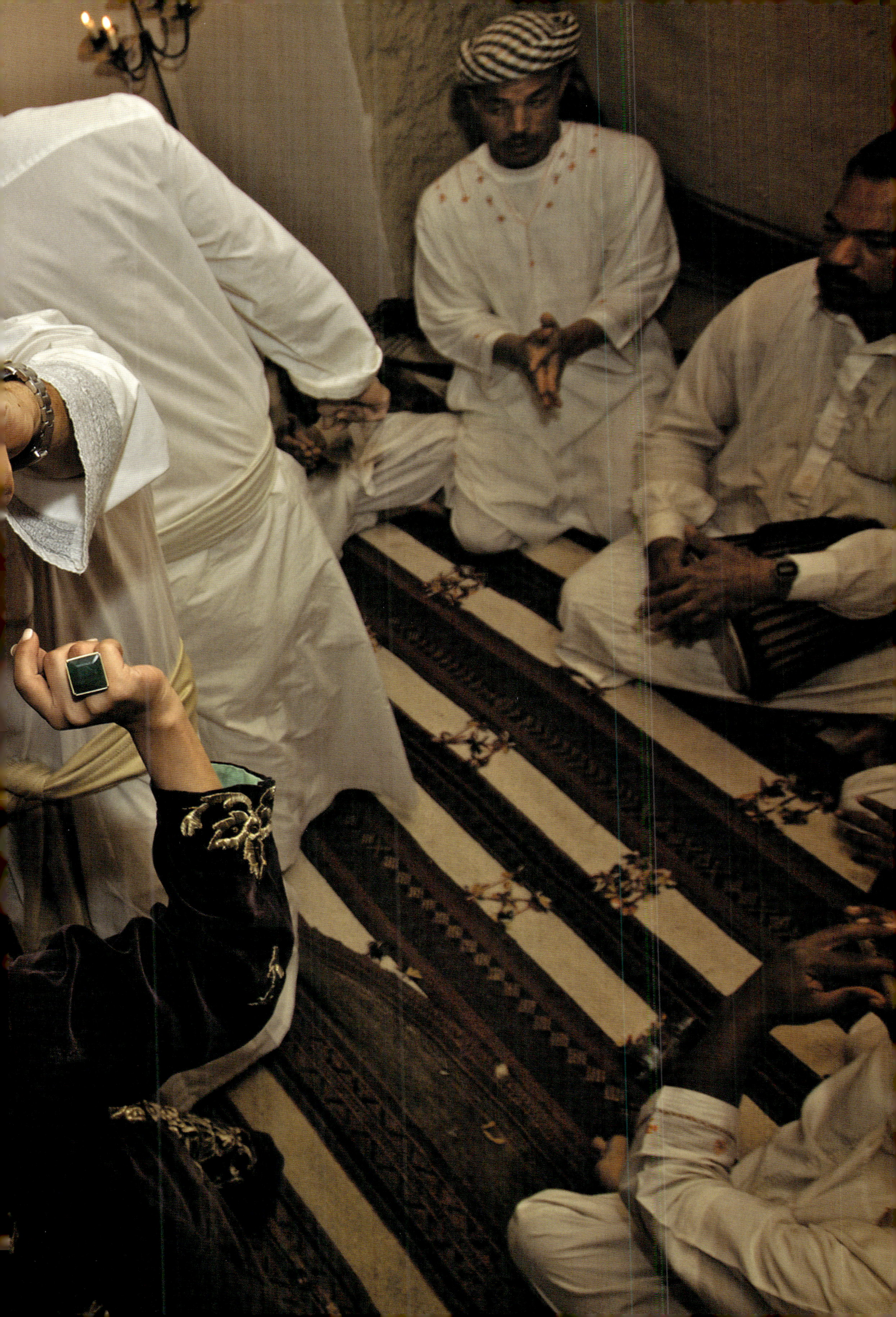

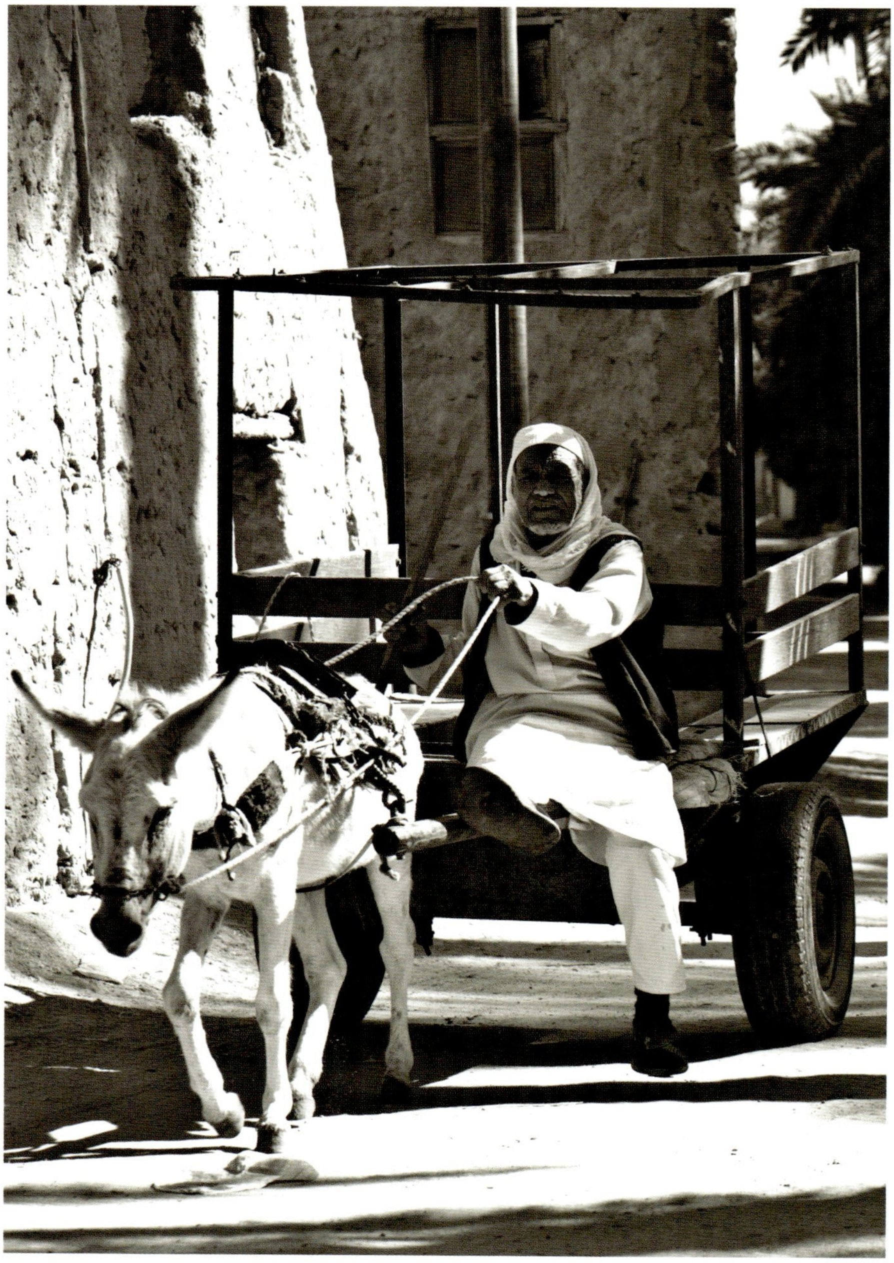

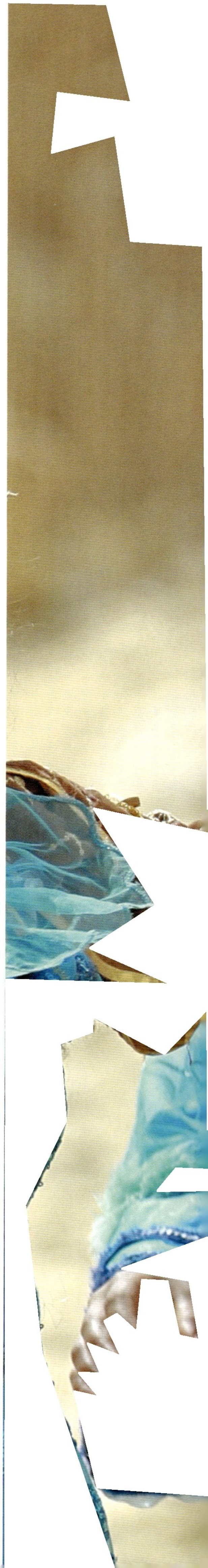

An old man (opposite) leads his donkey cart to the town center;
only recently have motor vehicles become a common sight in Siwa
Girls in 'special' clothes for the celebrations of the Siyaha festival

RAFIC SAID
Financier, Siwa homeowner (with wife Hana Helmy)

MY FATHER TRAVELS TO SIWA SEVERAL TIMES A YEAR WITH FAMILY AND FRIENDS. WHEN HE FIRST ASKED ME TO ACCOMPANY HIM 15 YEARS AGO, I ADMIT THAT THE PROSPECT OF A LONG, TIRING TRIP TO THIS TINY DOT IN THE SAHARA DID NOT FILL ME WITH JOY. IT WAS AN ADVENTURE, HOWEVER, AND ONE THAT I WOULD MAKE BY HIS SIDE. IT TURNED OUT TO BE ONE OF HIS GREATEST GIFTS TO ME.

Now each time I return, the distance and discomfort of the passage only heightens my anticipation. Contrasting feelings of excitement and calm creep in, as the dunes rise before your eyes and you catch the fleeting glimmer of the salt-pan on your approach.

On arrival you are arrested by beauty, struck with awe as if entering a place of mystical reverence. A feeling of utter tranquility floats towards you, and a deep inhalation of that cleansing air brings a broad and peaceful smile across your face.

Daily life in Siwa is simple but utterly fulfilling. In the morning, after awaking from sublime slumber on a bed cast in salt crystal, you might float, limbs lolling, across the lake, entirely supported by its saltiness, cleansing your skin of city toxins with the curative mud beneath. In the afternoon, you can gallop across the desert on a beautiful stallion with the acceleration of a sports car.

At night no neon lights, no manufactured music, just the flickering of candles and the sounds of the desert as you enjoy an exquisite, locally sourced, fresh organic dinner.

It is truly a place of enlightenment, and so I cannot put into words the joy I felt when my father redoubled this gift by presenting us with a villa in Siwa as a wedding present in 2009. The house is set on an elevated piece of land beneath the White Mountain, Adrere Amellal. The lake pans out ahead while surrounding palm trees cool it in the midday heat.

Our neighbor is old friend and sage Dr Mounir Neamatalla in his Tamazid villa, a man instrumental in the restoration and preservation of Siwa. He designed our house with direction from prominent architect and designer India Mahdavi, whose appreciation for linear structures and volume influenced its final appearance. It combines the mud-brick method of building native to Siwa, with a streamlined, modern aesthetic. Simple living and clean thinking.

Ahead of our wedding, Hana and I invited forty loved ones to join us in Siwa for preemptive recuperation before the mad whirl of festivities that was to follow back in Cairo. Young and old (from six months to 88 years old) were loaded onto the coach, chattering excitedly, few with any idea of what to expect. Moments of wonder followed, such as when a sand storm cleared and we found ourselves on the route through El Alamein. Sir Ronald Grierson, a senior advisor at the company I work for and a key confidant, took the microphone and guided us through his last visit to this place, when he served with the Allied forces in 1942.

Several hours later, the look of sheer amazement on the faces of dear friends as we approached the dunes, is an image I shall never forget.

My father understands the concept of inner peace, and through Siwa he has imparted this way of life to me. I am forever grateful that he brought me to this hallowed place and allowed me the opportunity, in turn, to introduce it to others.

Rafic Said's villa, seen from a distance beneath White Mountain (below), combines traditional mud brick with a modern, linear aesthetic

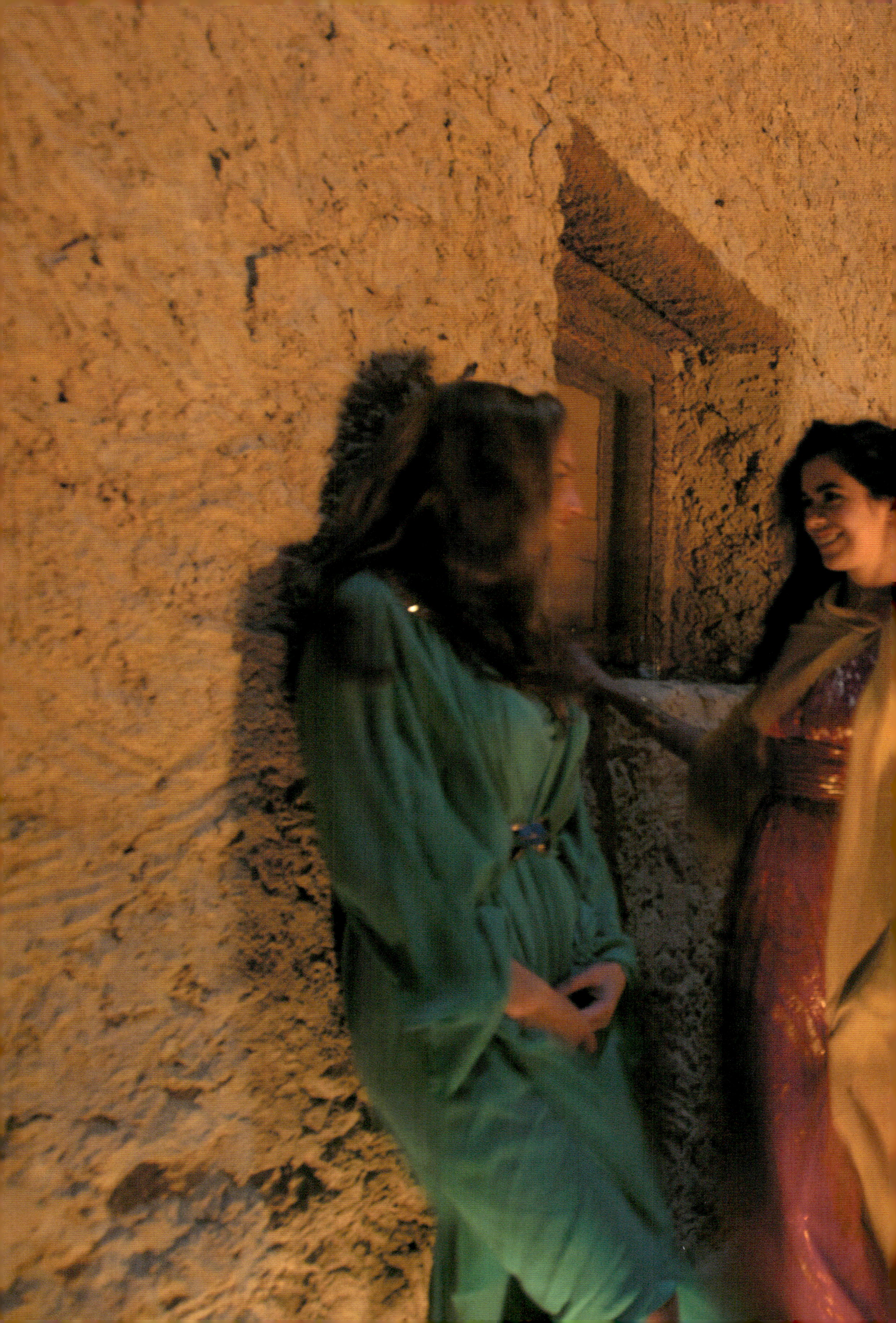

Rafic's wife, Hana, entertains friends and family in the courtyard of their house; only candles, stars, and an outdoor fire-pit light up the spaces around them

A lone dirt road leads the way to White Mountain and the discreet properties that surround it

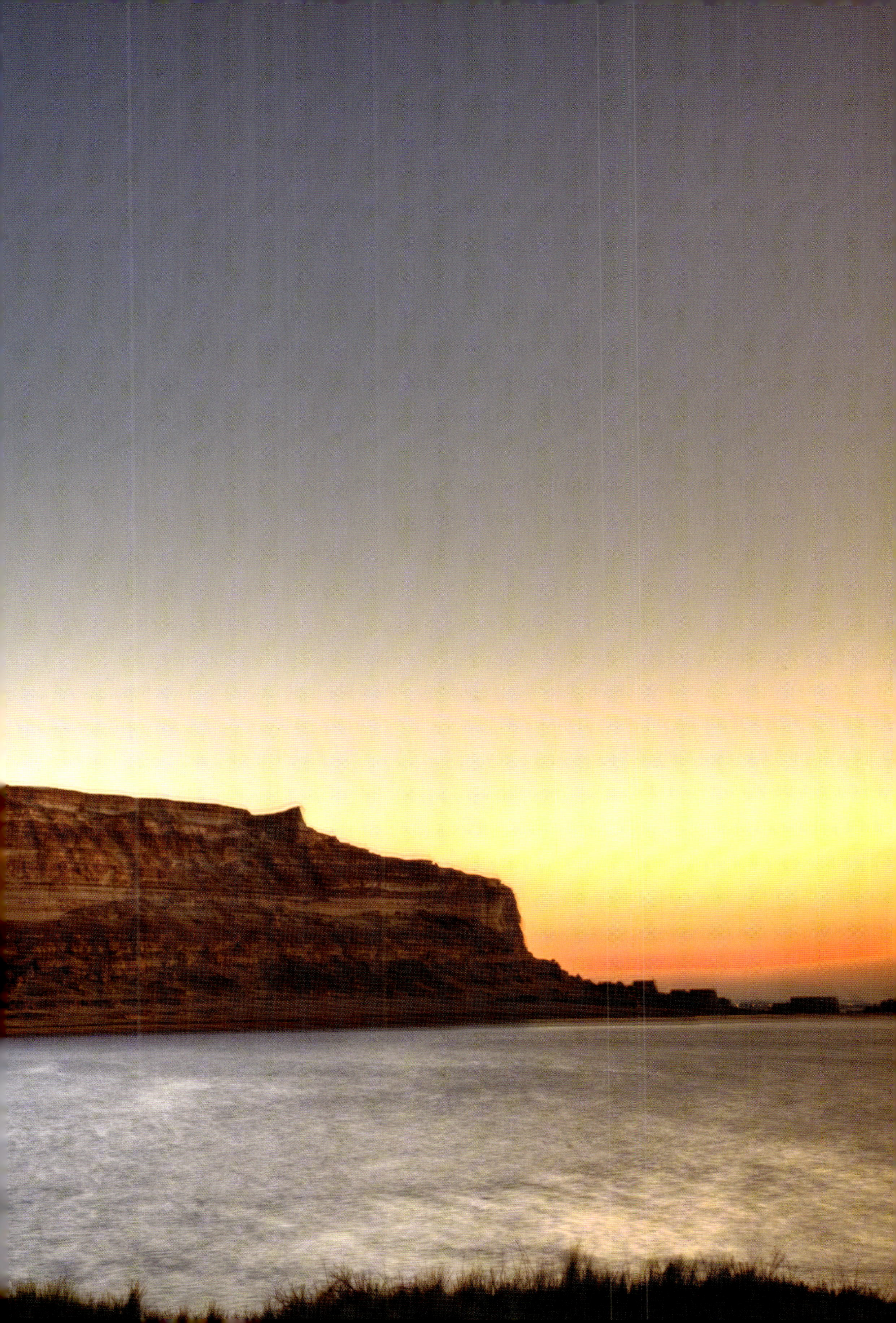

The Sahara can be enjoyed on horseback; experienced riders relish the chance to race across the sand at top speed

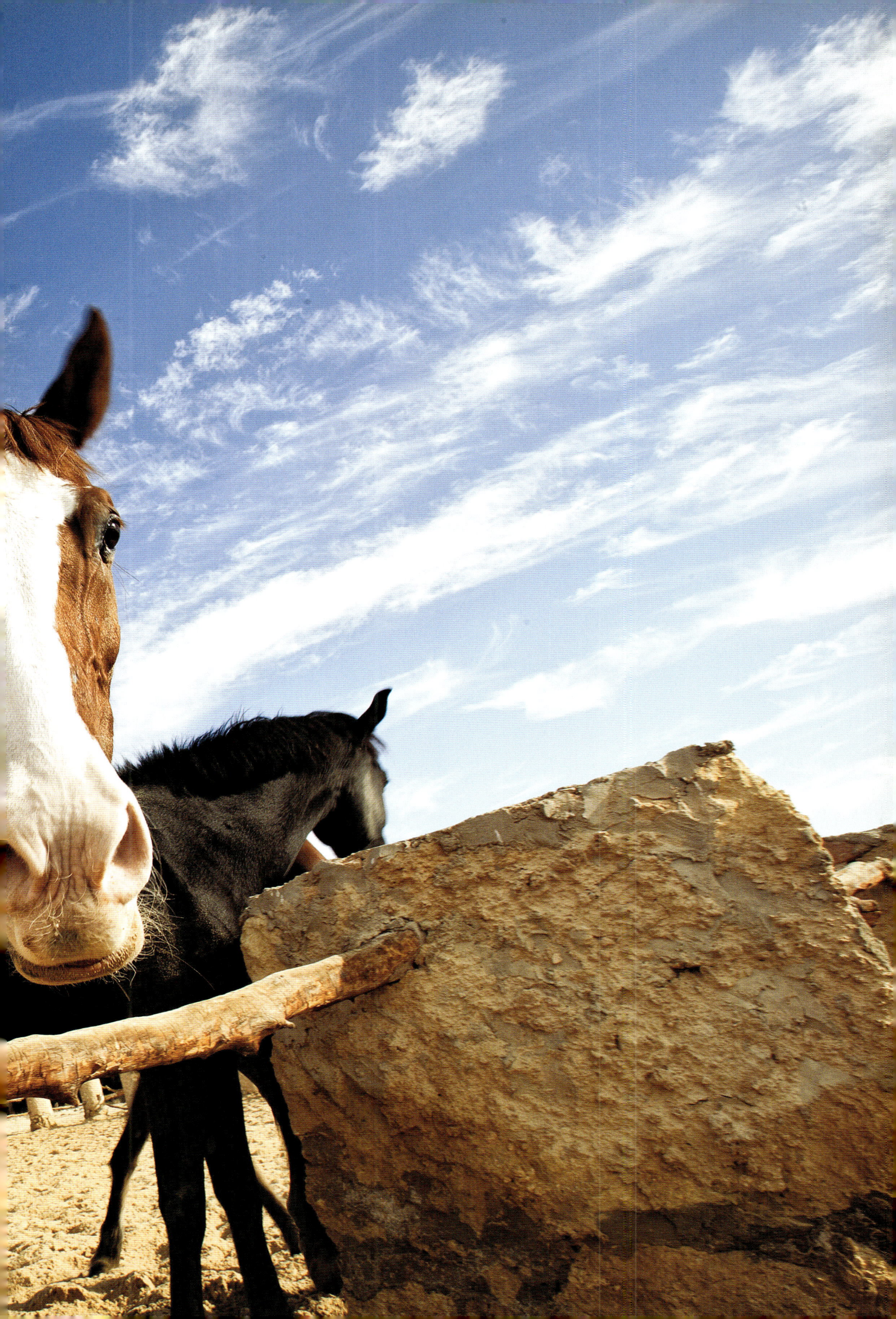

A staffer at Al Babenshal boutique hotel in the town center lights a fireplace in the lounge

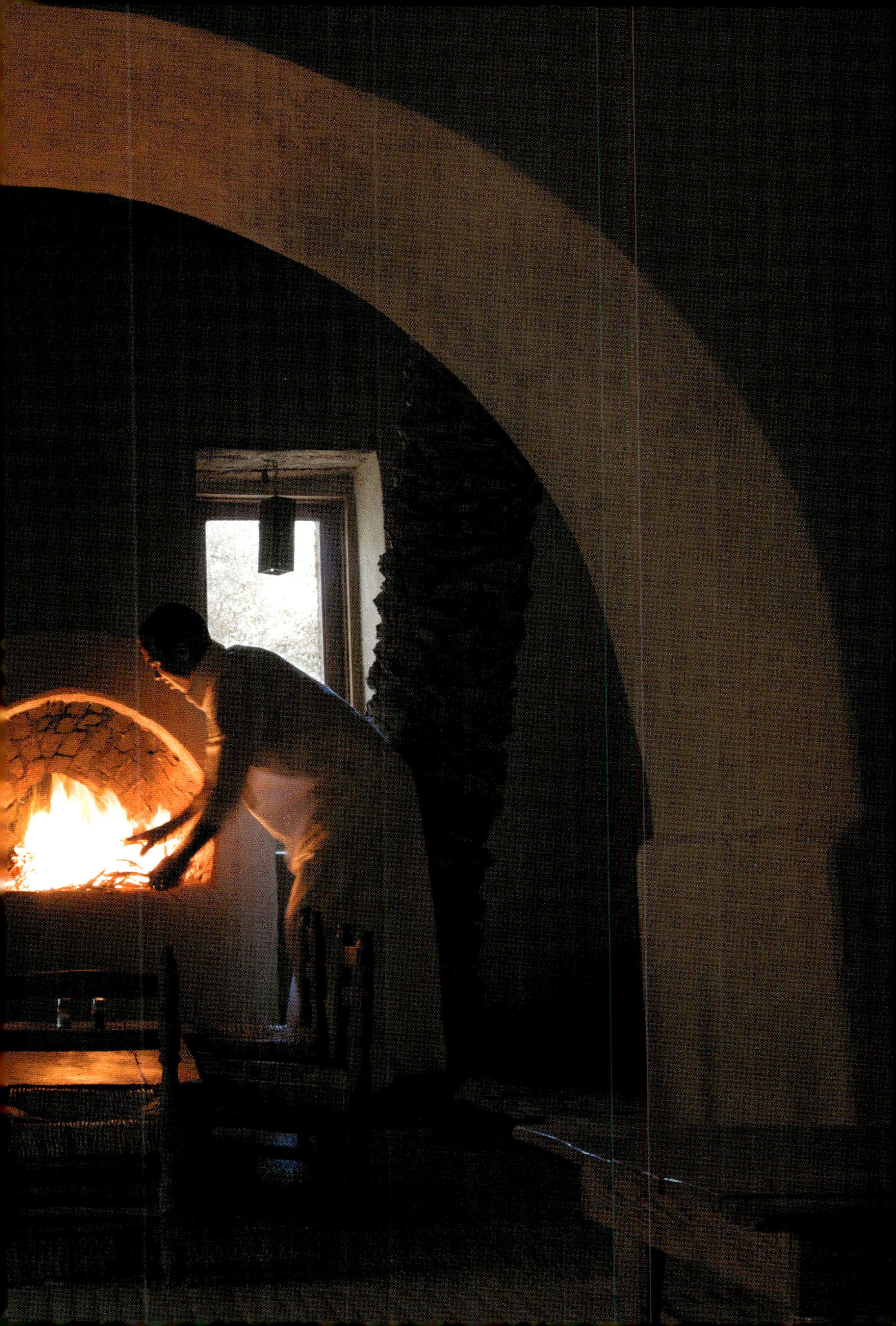

INSPIRATIONS

FROM

SIWA

Art
Jewelry & Costume
Décor
Cuisine

ART

Adel El-Siwi
Reverse Pilgrimage

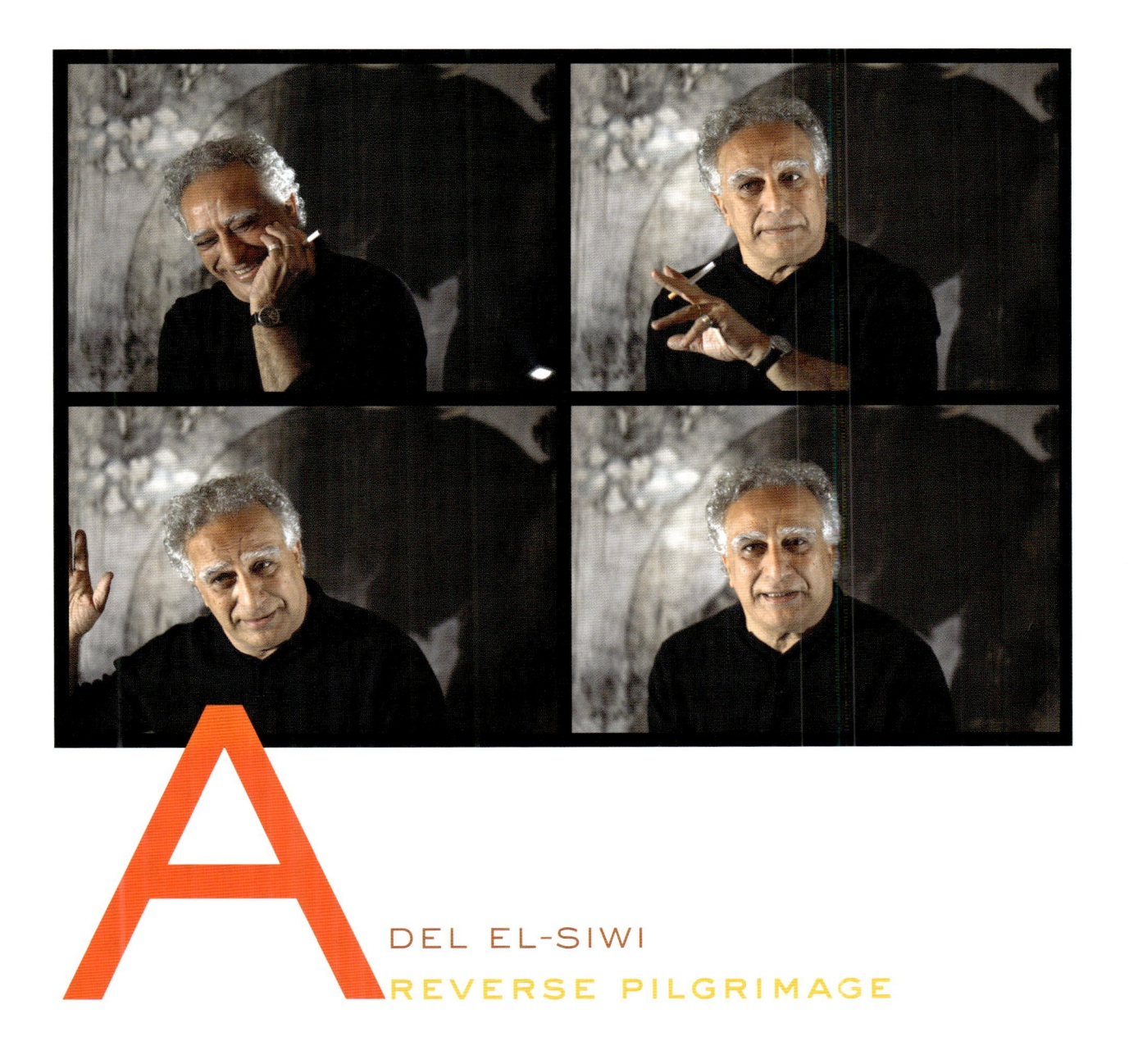

Adel El-Siwi is one of the masters of Egypt's contemporary art movement. His studio in downtown Cairo is a Pandora's box of old photographs, memorabilia and of course magnificent works of art. On a closer look, however, there are little clues; insignificant at first, but when examined closely, revealing more about the artist's history and sentimentality. On his coffee table, next to a packet of cigarettes, is a small box of dates from Siwa store El-Jawhara. On the bathroom wall, there is a black-and-white photograph of a handsome dark donkey. By the computer is a photograph of an older, distinguished gentleman, his father most likely. This artist is not from around here.

The art in the studio is rich, textural, colorful and speaks volumes about how deeply influenced Adel El-Siwi is by the notion of cultures, ethnicities and history. His art is not restrained; instead it always seems to over-extend, casting long shadows of meaning. When Adel El-Siwi describes his art, there is an undercurrent of nostalgia. The irony is that this nostalgia is not based on memory—after all, Adel El-Siwi never actually lived in Siwa as an adult. But his journey as an artist has ignited in him a sense of longing for the place of his ancestral heritage. On a quiet Wednesday evening in January, he talks about the idea of a reverse pilgrimage to Siwa. This is what he says:

The oasis is my home. I was born in Beheira in 1952. My family moved around freely between the various oases in the Western Desert, and settled in a small spot near Siwa. This is typical of desert tribes and we were no exception. I have almost no memory of life in the oasis because my father brought us to Cairo when I was very little. Growing up, I forgot about the whole thing, completely swept away by my studies, art and trips abroad. Many years later, after I returned to Cairo to live and work, with my Italian wife, my father chastised me for abandoning Siwa.

So I took a trip out there with my wife and daughter. I remember sitting in Abdou's Café for lunch. When the bill came I noticed we had been overcharged. I took the bill to Abdou himself to complain, making it a point to tell him that I was from Siwa. He glanced at my wife and daughter and asked, "And are they supposed to be from Siwa, too?" I was amused by his audacity; Siwans were never ones to mince their words. I told him about my tribal lineage and went into detail about the family's background. He must have still been skeptical about my claims because a few hours later, a delegation from my tribe appeared at the hotel to see me. When we met they asked all kinds of questions; I suppose they wanted to make sure I was who I claimed to be. Once they had confirmed my identity their entire demeanor changed: they became warm and said with a certain relief, "We've been looking for you for years! We had no idea where you were or how to find you!" It was an emotional moment with a group of people I did not know, but who for some reason felt like they could have been my brothers.

That was how it all started. In subsequent trips to Siwa I became consumed with the idea of building a home there, a place I could return to often. I own some land by Jaafar Mountain and every time I visit I am overwhelmed by how beautiful it is. I sometimes imagine building an artists' guesthouse there, a place where my peers and I could go for a creative retreat, to paint and relax. It would be a simple mud-brick house, in the authentic Siwa style, and I would have a large garden for my palm and olive trees. The younger generation of El-Siwis would have a chance to visit and reconnect with the place they only heard about from family gatherings. This image keeps coming back to me in my dreams. I feel inexplicably drawn to it.

The nostalgia I feel appears often in my art. Egypt is so diverse that there is always a story to be told by someone, a place they left behind, a memory. In my art I have African, Islamic and Arab influences. The multicultural heritage of Egypt is my inspiration and the art movement is stronger because of it. I am particularly moved by the dignity in the physical attitudes of, say, farmers in the countryside or nomads in the desert. They have a distinctive quality and pride I do not see in the urban population. Perhaps in the city the youth are too oppressed by materialistic fervor; it can be humiliating to fall behind the rest. In the countryside, however, in the desert, or by the Delta, nature's bounty and community life is a purveyor of strength, so that even in poverty men and women have a profound sense of dignity and self-worth.

Despite all the multicultural references in my work, I have no art that draws from the oasis or its Berber dwellers, but it remains the place I yearn for the most. It is a little ironic I know, but it may be something I will be able to explain a few years from now. Until then there is still so much to do with my art, and my studio is my home. I feel safe within its walls, lifted by its energy.

I have little mementos here and there that remind me of places and people that mean something to me. I keep them close at hand, as one would a talisman. I know how fortunate I am to be doing the one thing I love the most in life. That doesn't mean that there aren't a few more things out there that I long for. Some days I forget about them, other days they are all I can think about.

I have traveled so much in my life, and yet it is the road to Siwa that is the most elusive.

The Princess
317x147cm, mixed media on canvas, 2008/10

Face of a Young Woman
120x100cm, mixed media on canvas, 2010/11

The Woman With the Blue Earrings
120x10 cm, mixed media on canvas, 2010/11

JEWELRY & COSTUME

Guests at Adrere Amellal lounging in kaftans produced by Siwan women, designed by Laila Nakhla

Laila Nakhla emerges after checking on her store; the costume and jewelry are of her own design

LAILA NAKHLA

EMPOWERING SIWAN WOMEN THROUGH THE ANCIENT ART OF EMBROIDERY

Walking through Siwa's town center, the colorful bustle of everyday life is in full throttle as shop keepers, vendors and café owners open their doors to locals and visitors. Donkey carts shuffle across the small roads, side by side with cars and bicycles. European backpackers browse local crafts as screaming schoolchildren run past them, pleased that school is out for the day. A young man, no older than 18, will be busy convincing newcomers to rent a donkey carriage for an afternoon of sightseeing. The barber shop is full of clients with their eyes on the small, blurry TV set. It is a familiar scene, except there is one missing element: women.

Married women in Siwa are the hidden, mysterious layer of society that rarely appears. They spend most of their time inside their homes, and if forced to go out it is always brief. Unmarried women busy themselves with education or work until they are chosen for marriage, an event they all aspire to, regardless of what talents they may have. Their career after marriage is inside the house and bearing children. A woman who does not marry lives a low-key life with a father or brother, with little to do except housework.

This is the social fabric that Laila Nakhla contended with when she took on the enormous task of working with Siwan women on embroidery and textiles—a venture that by her own admission was entirely accidental. She used the local landscape and traditional costume and jewelry as inspiration for her pieces, which pay homage to Siwa while also making for a wearable and modern collection. Here is her story. An enchanting tale of creative collaborations and empowering women:

Siwa is renowned within Egypt for its traditional costume and jewelry, and so I was very excited on my first trip there to see the women in full regalia and to examine their embroidery techniques. When I got there in 1997 I was shocked to discover that these ancient arts had died out completely. The market was saturated with badly stitched, poor-quality outfits in polyester. The new generation of Siwan women did not know how to embroider in the tradition of their grandmothers, and there was no place where they could learn.

I had no intention of doing anything about it at that time. I was not a designer by background. I had experience designing jewelry through the *Nakhla* brand that my husband had started. As for clothing, I had been designing kaftans to wear myself because I found them so comfortable and had little interest in the voluminous, busy versions available in Cairo. My 'modern' kaftans, designed simply and with a more streamlined silhouette, received much media attention and with the insistence of my brother, Mounir Neamatalla, I was asked to revive the embroidery industry in Siwa. A tall order!

My objective sounded simpler than it was: I would use traditional Siwan costumes and embroidery techniques as inspiration to produce a new breed of modern, high-quality clothing that would appeal to contemporary markets. To do that, however, I had to find a way to teach young Siwan women how to embroider in the traditional style. The only people who had that knowledge and skill were the Siwan grandmothers.

With the help of a small British grant dedicated to training women, I approached the grandmothers and asked them if they would agree to teach embroidery to a total of five women each in return for a fee. The answer was always the same: we are busy in the mornings with household chores, and in the afternoons we cannot see. I was thoroughly confused; these women lived in homes with electricity and light and yet they all claimed they couldn't see in the afternoons. Was this an inside joke or a play on words? It eventually dawned on me what the problem was and I had to laugh; the grandmothers were all shortsighted, and the tight stitch of the embroidery was too difficult for them to see in the milder light of the afternoons! The next day I set out and bought dozens of optical glasses in a variety of lenses and distributed them to all the women. We were finally on our way.

Siwa is a small town and nothing stays a secret for long. Our driver there, Ali Tromai ("*tromai*" means straight like a tramway; in Siwa people often take on the name of their own finest quality and he was a level driver) had been quietly listening to the endless talk about training the women to embroider. One day he came over to me with a rectangular strip of cotton fabric, divided into four sections. Each section had a different motif, including the palm tree and olive tree. He said it was a sample of work by his unmarried daughter, Ne'ma, who lived with him at home. It was absolutely lovely but most of all, it was *inspired*. It was as if she had summarized my entire mission on a single strip of fabric. Without ever having met or spoken to her, I knew I had found the woman who could help me take the project from casual in-house training to organized workshops. I hired her right away as the manager and Chief Embroiderer of the first Women's Workshop. I opened the workshop next door to her father's house so that she could commute easily and work in a family-friendly environment where she felt comfortable.

It was in Siwa, with my women embroiderers, that Toni Scervino, of Italian fashion house Ermanno Scervino, developed and produced four years of summer collections starting in 2003. I still remember working with him under a solitary lightbulb, in a small space beneath Shali Lodge in town. He was impressed with the discipline and talent of the women, and knew that the genre of handmade detailed stitching they provided could not be emulated anywhere in Italy. From clothes we expanded organically into other product lines. For example, when my women got married they left the workshop, so I came up with the idea of producing tablecloths and sheets because, unlike clothing, they took 45 days to make. This meant married women could be assigned the longer jobs at home, while the unmarried women worked on the high-turnover items with short deadlines at the workshop. I even hired a married woman who was responsible for allocating and collecting jobs assigned to other married women. In other words, instead of attempting to change the way the women lived, we adapted the business to their needs. I became the bridge between the women and the outside world. My responsibility was to train them, give them designs and assignments, then sell their work. I am proud to say their collections are sold in Siwa, Cairo, Europe and the Americas.

A dear friend of mine, Marie Assad, now in her 90s, had a long career working with women in community-based programs. I once complained to her about the difficulty of working in a society where women's mobility, freedom and self-development was so limited. It made for a frustrating business model with a high staff turnover. She was unexpected in her response; she said, "Don't get carried away, or try to lead a revolution!" Instead of provoking the sensibilities of an old society, Marie recognized the benefits of engaging the heads of the households—the fathers, brothers and husbands—so that they too benefited in some way from the women having jobs. In so doing, the women's careers become a source of pride rather than shame, and their empowerment all-inclusive. At the same time, she asked me to reaffirm to my women the sanctity of the household, and encourage them to thank their fathers and brothers for allowing them to work and earn. This, she said, would go much further than waging sociological warfare. And she was right.

My clothing line today takes inspiration from old-school embroidery, mimicking its tiny stitch and focus on quality. In my designs I departed from the limited color scheme of traditional Siwan costume, introducing all kinds of pop colors that I felt would look beautiful against the monochromatic background of the desert. The small motifs would be added in a very subtle way, but by far and wide it is the olive tree motif that remains the favorite. My lines are always simple, so that wearing the kaftans, in their various lengths, is comfortable and flattering. I also produce shirts and warm wraps with the same focus on tiny stitching and detail overlaying an inherently modern design.

With jewelry, I had to reinvent things entirely. Traditional jewelry as a craft had disappeared and antique pieces were

Laila Nakhla's coveted "salt" necklaces, combined here with lava, silver engraved in the ancient Siwan tradition and semi-precious stones

hard to find. A European couple had bought pieces in bulk before I arrived in Siwa, smuggling them back to Europe to be sold there. I had no desire to emulate ancient jewelry pieces, not only because I could not possibly produce pieces in the same manner, but also because they were very ornate and difficult to wear. Heavy pieces hanging from hair or necks would simply not be worn by today's generation, especially since my customers are outside Siwa and generally foreign. I took my cue from the earth, using salt, Siwa's abundant resource, in my necklaces and mixing it with semi-precious and colorful gems. I even added embroidery on leather, mounted on silver. The result is modern, but a closer look shows the subtle Siwan influence, and the nod to its nature.

My work with Siwan women was a personal odyssey in community work and cooperation. I got to know them all as people, not just as employees in a workshop. I witnessed first-hand the skill and determination these women had and their joy at having a profession that would give them financial independence and a sense of self-worth.

Ne'ma, my right-hand manager and embroiderer, ended up getting married later than usual. She married a like-minded partner who had just returned from the big city and who valued Ne'ma's professional achievements and maturity. Today, in the world of international embroidery, Ne'ma is a recognized name—no small feat for a woman from Siwa.

DÉCOR

LOCAL MASTER CRAFTSMEN PRODUCE WORLD-CLASS PRODUCTS

The most popular man in Siwa goes by the name Haboub. He is a large man, well over six feet tall, and can tell you stories about Siwa and its people all day long. He is Dr Mounir Neamatalla's go-to man for supervising the ecolodge, particularly where it relates to staff and supplies. He has seven children; when he finally fathered a boy after many girls, he named him after his youngest brother who had died from a sudden illness at 15. His brother's dying wish had been for Habcub to name a son after him. And he did: today little Mostafa is a mischievous addition to the house.

Haboub whips us around Siwa in one of Adrere Amellal's safari jeeps. Along the way he tells us about a man in Qara oasis who believes the palm tree has 96 benefits. He cannot remember each benefit, but they are all wonderful, he says, for helping the body and mind. Around town various shops sell dates, so we stop at one recommended to us (El-Jawhara) and pick up two boxes of dates stuffed with almonds. We also stop at the shop at the Babenshal boutique hotel to buy organic olive oils, jams and dressings from their delightful Siwa Organics line. Right outside we chat with the infectiously charming Salama, whose café has become something of an institution for visitors looking for a tasty local meal.

Our real interest, however, is the craftsmen in their workshops. We have three on our tour: rope master Ahmed Ali, stone master Abdel Salam Ghanim, and salt master Sayed Aboul Kasem (whose story appeared with India Mahdavi's contribution). Three men with very different trades, but who share the same history: it was Dr Mounir Neamatalla who sponsored the launch of their businesses, in exchange for exclusivity deals with the ecolodge and its sister properties. It is difficult to see these men at work, in their various workshops and quarries, and not be moved by the benefits of promoting small, clever businesses that utilize natural resources in meaningful ways. We sit down for "Dhahwiya" or mid-morning snack with each of them. Over sweet tea, they speak candidly about their lives and work. They also insist that we tell them the exact date of our next visit to Siwa, because they want to see us again. Spending time with them and their assistants constitutes one of our finest days in Siwa. Here are their stories:

AHMED ALI
Rope Master

My father taught me all I know about the rope business. Back then we made rope products that were used for daily life in Siwa. We used rope for donkey carts, date picking and other day-to-day activities. It gave us a very modest living; we had trouble making ends meet.

My life as a Rope Master changed when I started working with Dr Mounir, because he expanded the product line and made it more of a commercial business. Suddenly, rope was being used to make all kinds of things, from household furniture to cladding ceilings and doorways. The options were endless, and showed us the hidden versatility of rope.

I worked with India Mahdavi, whose designs are always lovely. We make beautiful headboards from rope, and she has one of those in her Siwa home. We also take wooden Siwan chests and upholster them in rope. I design the patterns for the various assignments I am given.

I have two assistants who produce the rope for me. That way I can control the kind of rope I work with because sometimes I need a thin soft breed, other times the thicker coarser kind. The rope we get from Cairo is not good at all so I had to make the production in-house. My men are very good at turning around the raw material quickly.

I have a 13-year old son who often visits me at the workshop after school. When he does I give him a little task that involves rope-work and then leave the scene for a while. I observe him from afar and I notice that he enjoys what he is doing. I'm not sure if he plans to take over after me, but I hope he does. It's a good life.

Rope Master Ahmed's headboard 'upholstered' in rope and placed on a colorful Bedouin rug

Rope Master Ahmed Ali, busy with a new design in his workshop where he uses all kinds of rope for a variety of decorative items

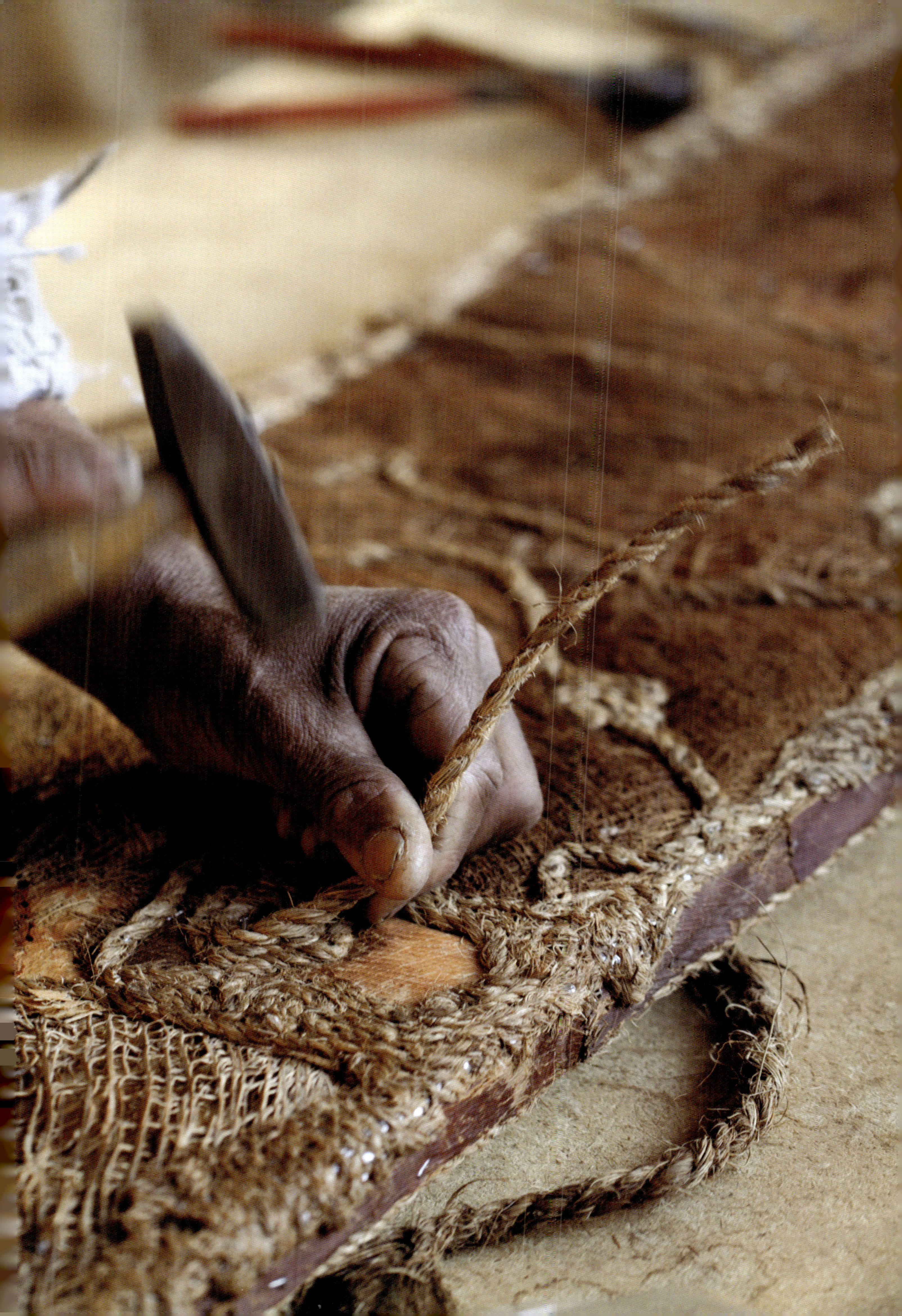

ABDEL SALAM GHANIM
Stone Master

I HAVE BEEN WORKING WITH STONE FOR 17 YEARS BUT IT DIDN'T START OUT THAT WAY. MY FIRST JOB WAS IN AN OLIVE FACTORY. I WOULD FINISH MY SHIFT AND GO TO THE QUARRY TO CARVE STONE AS A HOBBY. WITH TIME, THE "STONE CLUB" GREW IN NUMBER; WE WERE A BUNCH OF PEOPLE PRODUCING ALL KINDS OF THINGS, FROM TABLES TO ANIMAL FIGURES AND STATUES.

We would store everything we produced, hoping that one day they could be sold. It was a long shot; not many people in Siwa would spend their hard-earned money to buy a four-meter alligator made of stone.

So it was opportune that Dr Mounir found a market for our stone products. Now I have six people working with me, and Ben Driss is my right-hand man. Our quarry is in an area called Meshindit. It overlooks an old Pharonic quarry that was used long ago to build the Ancient Egyptian sites at Amun. We consider this auspicious and it gives us great energy at work.

My main products are tables, while decorative items include animal and human figures. India Mahdavi designed the tables I produced for the ecolodge. I used to make much chunkier tables, with surfaces starting at 15cm thick. India brought that thickness down to about 10cm, and though it looks much better it means we have to work with more precision when manufacturing and transporting the tables.

I have to be present if any of my tables need to be moved from one spot to another; I'm a bit controlling that way.

Four years ago, I was riding my motorcycle at night on my way home from the quarry. It was pitch dark and I didn't see the donkey cart on the side of the road. It was a headlong collision and though nothing happened to the farmer or his donkey, I was seriously hurt. We do not have proper medical facilities in Siwa, so I had to go to Cairo for surgery. They told me my leg was broken, and I had to endure a cast for a long time. Throughout that unpleasant episode I remember fretting over not being at work with the boys, and it drove me a little mad to be honest.

Ben Driss and I have one wish: to visit Aswan and see the Pharonic sites there. Our Pharonic forefathers were the real stone masters, and we've heard so much about the magnificent stonework there. Dr Mounir said he would take us one day, but we are still waiting for him to make good on his promise. A Siwan never forgets!

Abdel Salam's partner, Ben Driss (above), looks on from the sunny outdoor stone quarry where the men work

An apprentice rises to the awesome challenge of crushing stone at the quarry

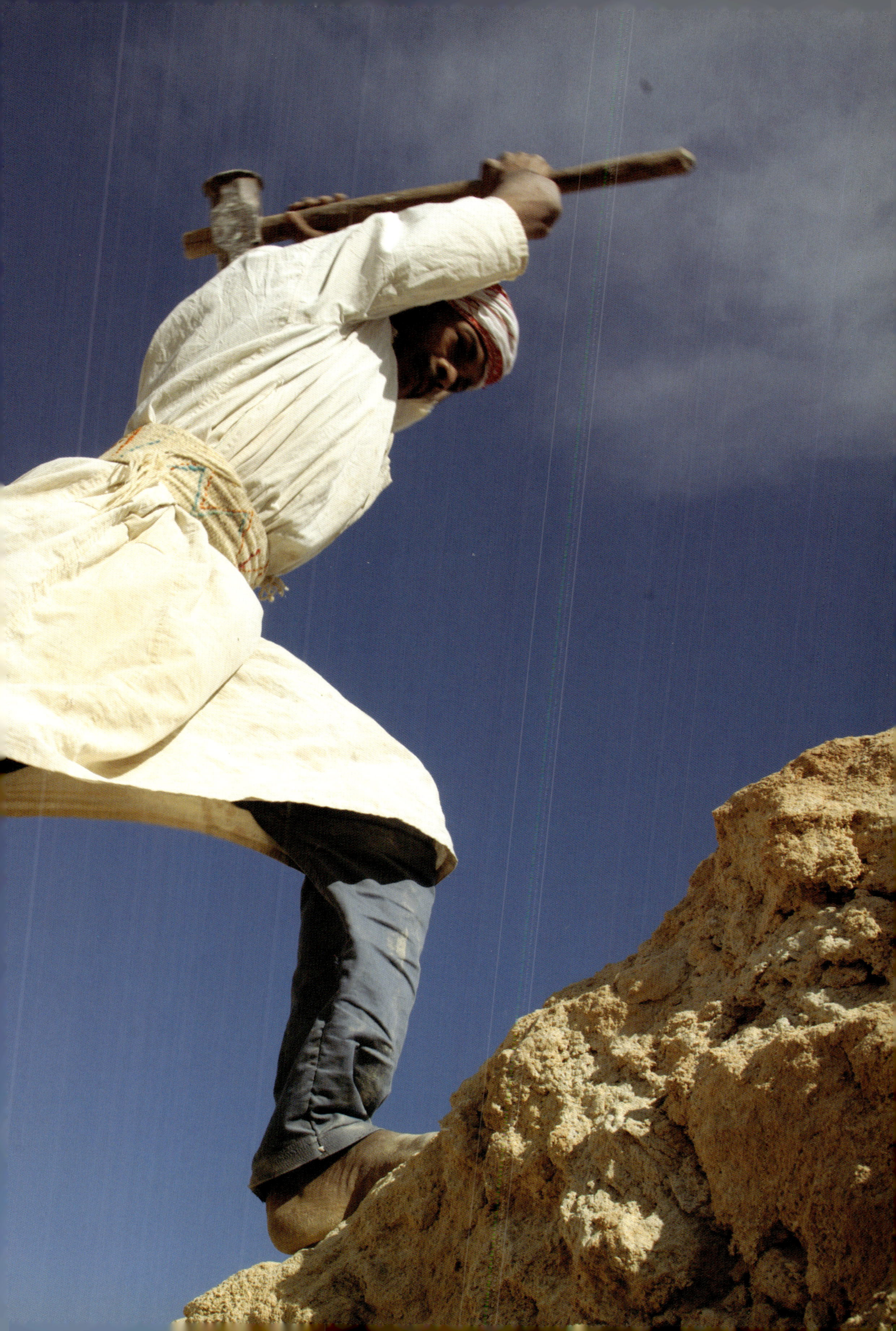

CUISINE

ADRERE AMELLAL CREATES A KITCHEN OF MODERN BERBER CUISINE

BERBER CUISINE IS A PRODUCT OF ITS TOUGH, ISOLATED TERRAIN. THERE IS A HEAVY FOCUS ON DATES, OLIVES AND VEGETABLES PLANTED AROUND THE OASES. SIWA OILS, SYRUPS AND JAMS ARE SOLD AT SEVERAL SMALL SHOPS DOWNTOWN. MEAT IS MORE OF A RARITY; IT APPEARS ON SPECIAL OCCASIONS, COOKED WITH SPICES IN LARGE POTS TILL TENDER AND SERVED WITH RICE OR COUSCOUS. SEAFOOD DOES NOT FEATURE AT ALL, AND OVERALL VARIETY AND COOKING METHODS ARE LIMITED.

Dr Mounir Neamatalla had to approach the cuisine concept for Adrere Amellal with a high degree of inventiveness. How could he take the basic Berber diet and modernize it, to give it depth and an element of surprise? With Head Chef Atef at the helm, he developed a creative and sublime menu that sources fresh organic vegetables from the ecolodge's own herb and vegetable gardens, and blends them into a cuisine that mixes the Berber palate with influences from Europe. The result is a dining experience that simply cannot be found anywhere else in the world.

Guests at the lodge anticipate each meal with relish. Breakfast is a hearty affair, often featuring *baid bil agga* (eggs cooked with dates), delicious jams made from olives and figs, and Egyptian *foul* (fava beans) served with Arabic bread in individually-sized clay pots. All the earthenware at the lodge is made-to-order from Upper Egypt. The pots are glazed with egg yolk and molasses, in the Ancient Egyptian technique, then fired up. This process of glazing makes the earthenware non-porous and able to withstand open fires. It also keeps the food warm for longer, and the more the earthenware is used the better it gets.

Lunch is a vegetarian meal, produced from the delicious organic vegetables and fruits sourced nearby. The meals are not just bursting with flavor, but also rich in color and texture. Stuffed parcels of spinach with chopped beets, zucchini spaghetti with cilantro, whole fried tomatoes filled with spiced peas, or the now infamous hibiscus risotto, are some of the specialties that feature during lunch, a meal served under the cooling canopy of the palm groves. Dinner is an exquisite experience, served in a different area of the lodge each night. It could be on an open-air rooftop with White Mountain looming overhead, or a medieval-inspired room with salt-encrusted walls and ceilings. Dinner can even be served in the middle of the Saharan dunes, as a fleet of the lodge's jeeps delivers simple tables, chairs and linens to set up a lounge and dining area on the fine sand. In all cases it is always candlelight, open fire pits and gas lanterns that illuminate, giving an ethereal, otherworldly feel. Naturally, guests are enchanted by the half-light, floating through the experience as though in a dream.

During dinner, either meat or duck is served with rice or couscous, after a vegetable starter. Salad as a third course is often wild rocket from the organic garden, served as simply as possible so that its peppery essence jolts and awakens the senses. Dessert is a beloved art form at Adrere Amellal: date cigars, date soufflé, *konafa* mini pies, and traditional *umm ali* bread pudding are all served with a slight divergence from conventional recipes. When Chef Atef emerges to bid farewell to guests on their final night, he is met with deafening applause.

A smile spreads across Dr Mounir's face, because theirs is a passionate collaboration, drawn from the bounty of the oasis, developed thoughtfully and with painstaking devotion to both tradition and novelty.

For the first time in their history, Adrere Amellal has agreed to part with the recipes of some of its most popular dishes. Organic ingredients should be sourced, where possible, to follow the ethos of Chef Atef's kitchen. Wear a colorful kaftan, play some tabla beats, open your kitchen to friends and family, serve in big clay pots and enjoy!

A farmer scales a palm tree during date picking season; the unmarried men who tended to palm trees and gardens in the past were a powerful group known as the "zaggalah"

Chef Atef Abdel Rahim
at Adrere Amellal ecolodge

Organic Tomatoes Stuffed with Herb Garden Peas

8 firm tomatoes with stems

½ kilo of fresh green peas

½ cup of fresh coriander, finely chopped

Sprinkle of dried coriander

1 small onion, finely chopped

1 tablespoon extra virgin olive oil

4 tablespoons of water

Salt and pepper to taste

FOR BATTER

1 teaspoon of baking powder

½ cup of all-purpose flour

Ladle of water

Oil for frying

Peel the tomatoes, keeping the stems and preserving some of the skin. Make a small hole at the base of the tomatoes and remove the seeds. Fry the onion in the oil until golden, then add the fresh coriander. Add the peas to the onion, mixing well for a few minutes before adding water. Season with the dried coriander, salt, and pepper. Simmer, covered, on low heat for 15 minutes. Remove and set aside.

Stuff the tomatoes with the pea mixture, sealing the opening with some of the reserved skin.

Prepare the batter by mixing the flour and baking powder. Whip the ingredients together while adding a ladle of water in intervals until you have a creamy consistency.

Dip the lower half of the tomato in the batter and fry until lightly browned.

Serve warm.

Serves 4

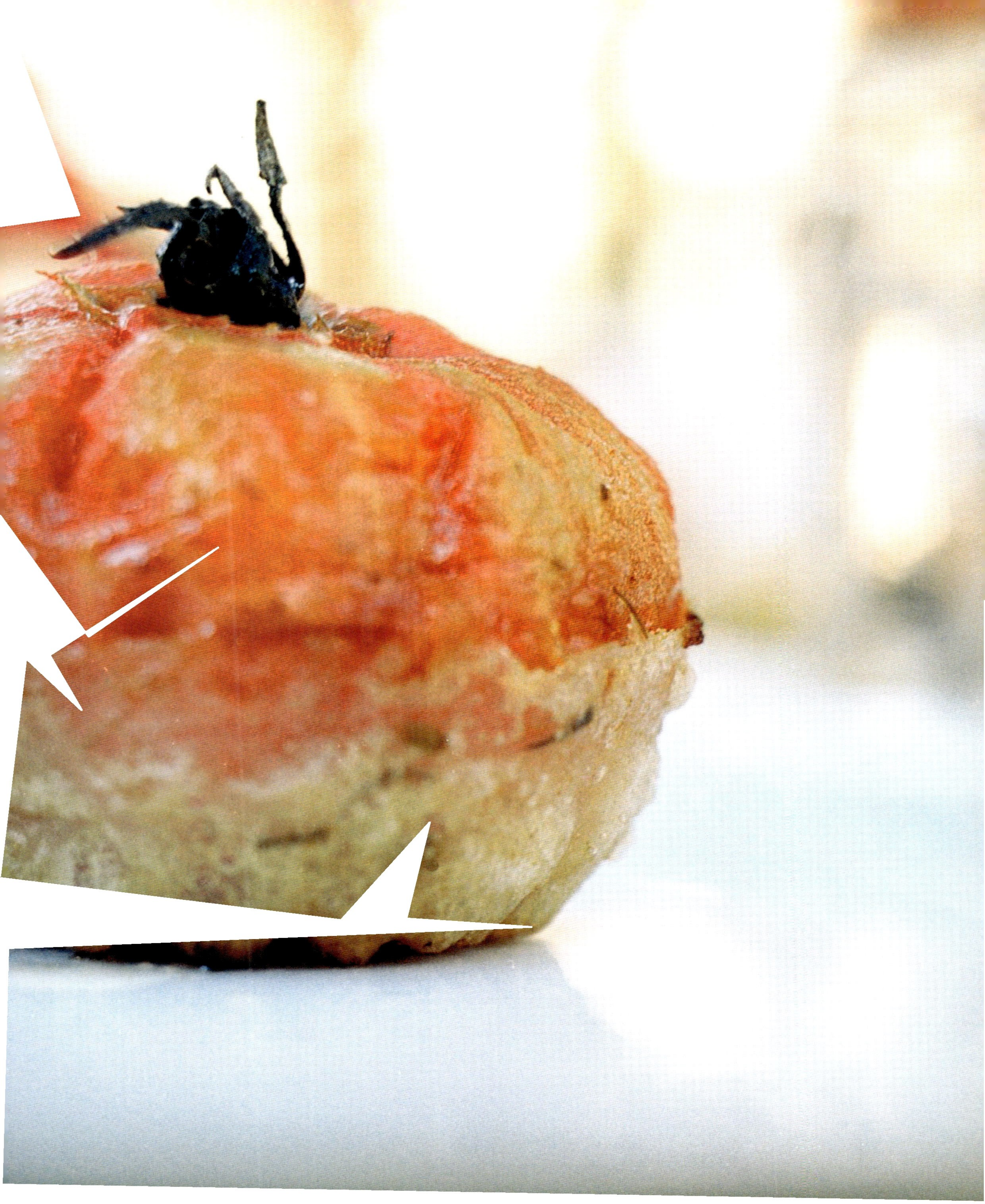

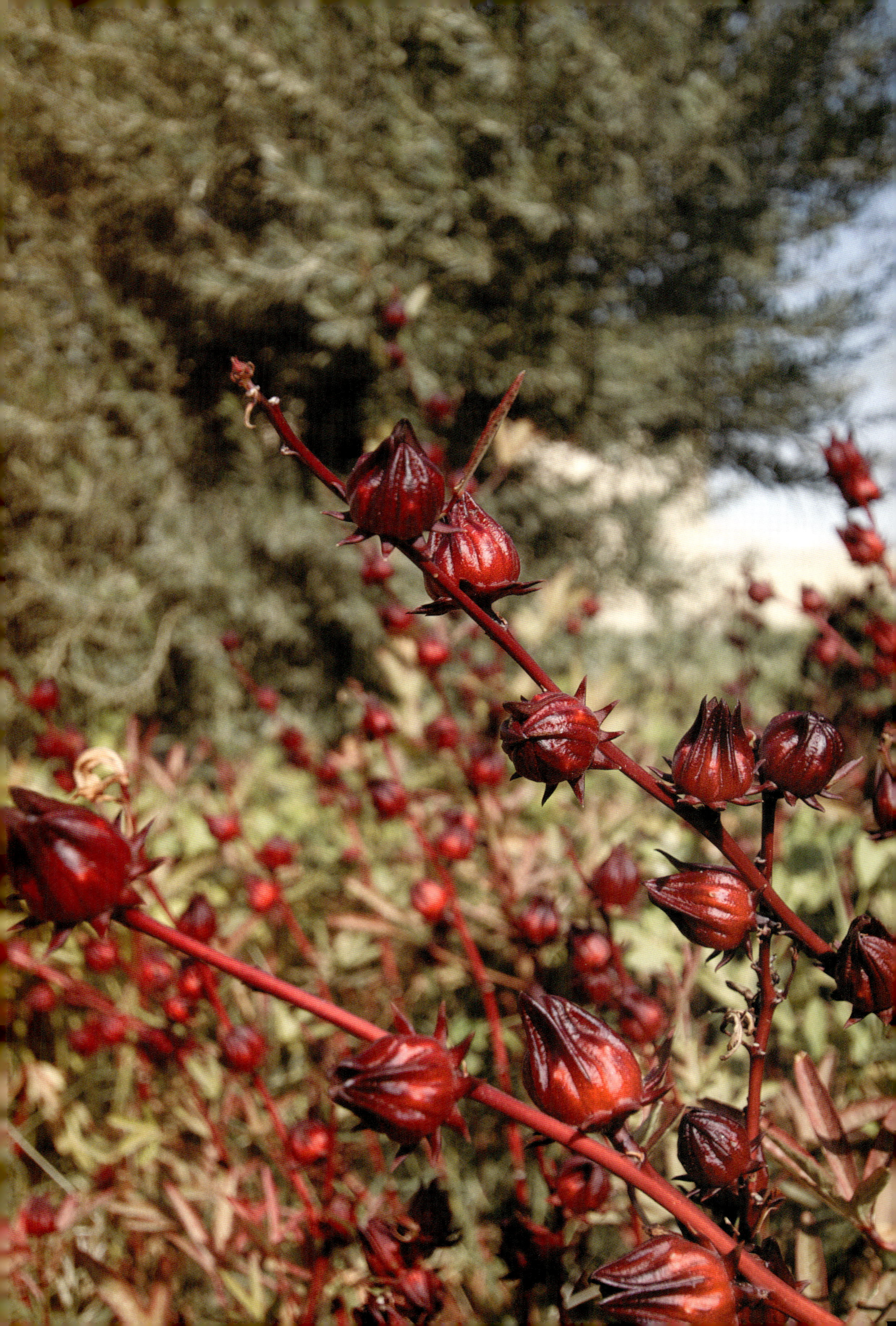

Hibiscus Risotto

Handful of hibiscus flowers

1 large onion, finely chopped

1 large boiled beetroot, peeled and cut into cubes

1 handful of small raisins

2 red apples, peeled and cut into cubes

½ cup of date syrup (or grape honey, found in specialty Middle Eastern stores)

3 cups of Arborio rice

6 tablespoons of butter

Grated Parmesan cheese

Soak the hibiscus flowers in 1.5 liters of cold water for an hour
Strain and set aside, reserving the colored water.

Heat a third of the butter in a casserole dish and add half the onions.
Sauté gently until browned. Add the raisins and syrup, mixing well.
Add the hibiscus water, beetroot and apples, and bring to the boil.
Cover and lower the heat to simmer.
This is the stock that will be used to cook the risotto.

In a separate casserole heat the remaining butter, then add the onions and sauté gently till browned. Add the rice and combine with the onion so that it becomes translucent, for around 5 minutes.
Add 2-3 ladles of hibiscus stock to the rice and stir well until absorbed.
Keep adding hibiscus stock in regular intervals, stirring well and allowing the rice to absorb the liquid throughout, until tender.
This should take around half an hour.
The rice should be soft but with a little bite, *al dente*, and and take on a rich mauve color.

Serve immediately with grated Parmesan on top.

Serves 6

Date Cigars

12 sheets of filo pastry

200 grams of date paste

Handful of nuts and almonds (optional)

Melted butter for pastry

Honey

Preheat the oven to 180°C.

Heat the date paste on low heat on its own until soft.
Add the mixture of nuts if preferred.
Spread the filo pastry on a work top and cut into segments 10cm wide.
Fold each sheet over, brush with butter and fold again.
Add around 1 tablespoon of date mixture in the center of the pastry and roll into a cigar shape. Once all done, put the "cigars" in a buttered oven-proof dish.

Bake in oven for 10 minutes until golden and crispy.

Serve drizzled with honey on top.

Serves 4

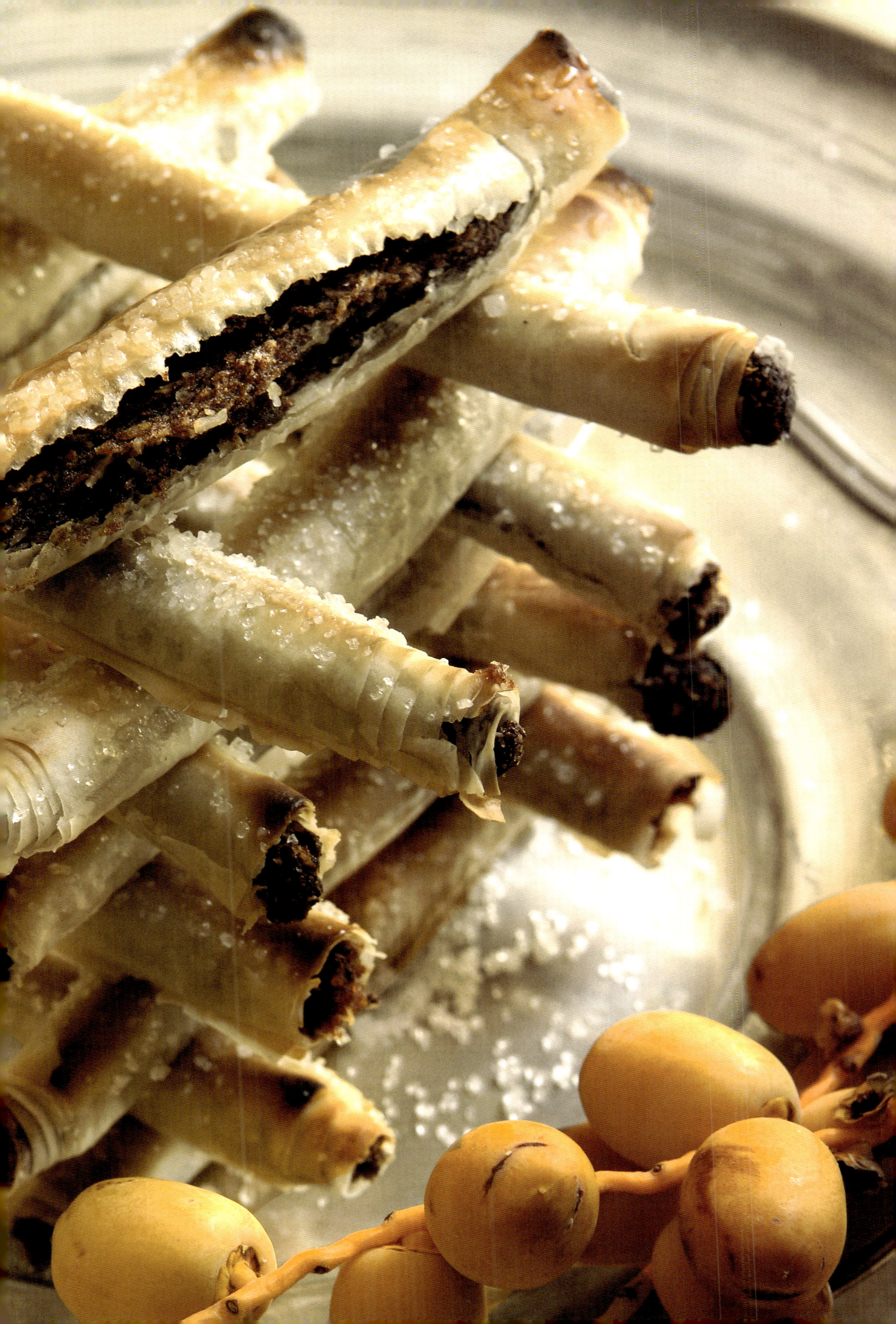

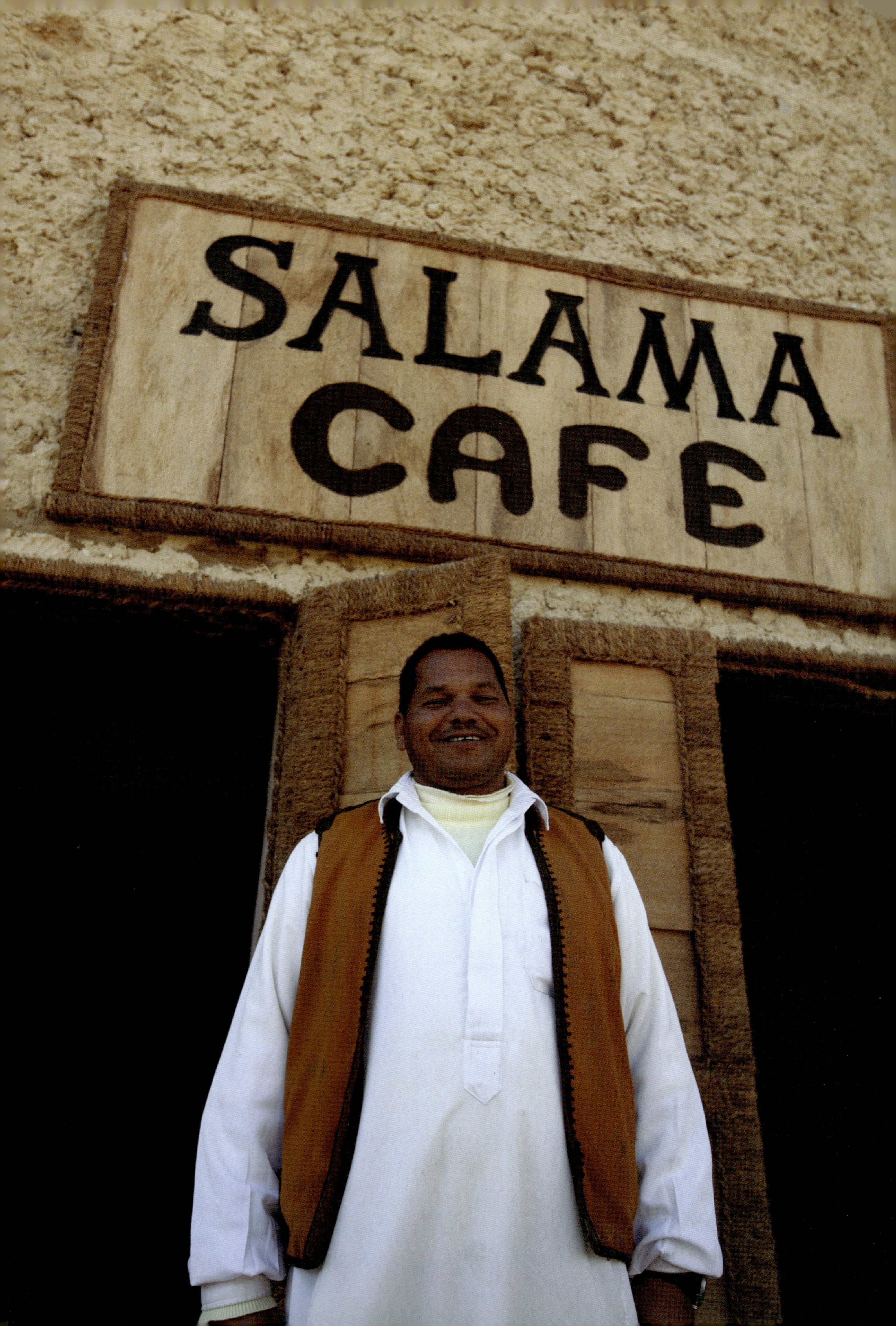
SALAMA
CAFE

Salama at the entrance of his popular café in the center of town that serves up tasty local fare
Oils and jams (below) displayed at the Siwa Organics shop by the Fortress of Shali entrance
Tribal headscarves in various colors and prints sold at the souk

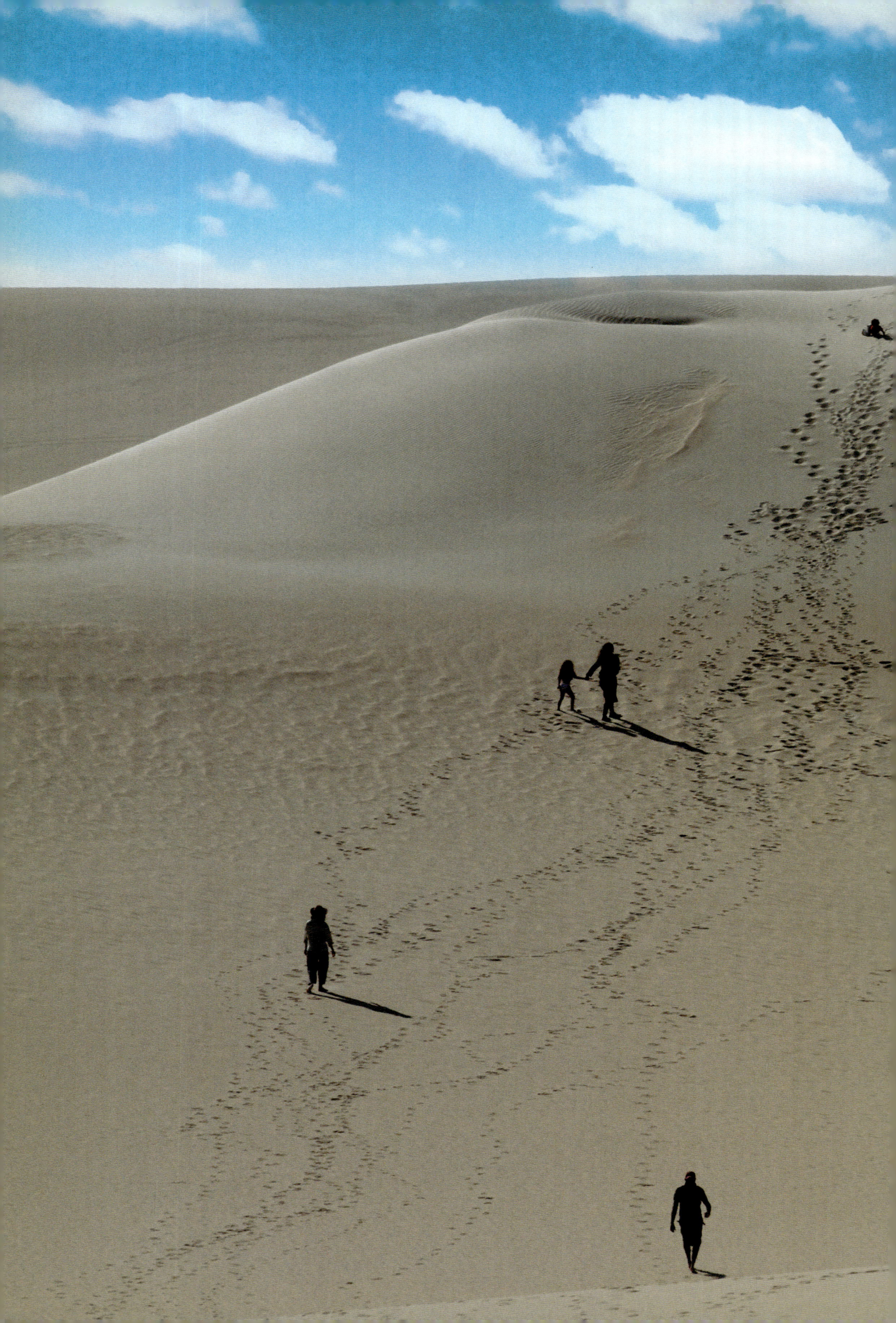

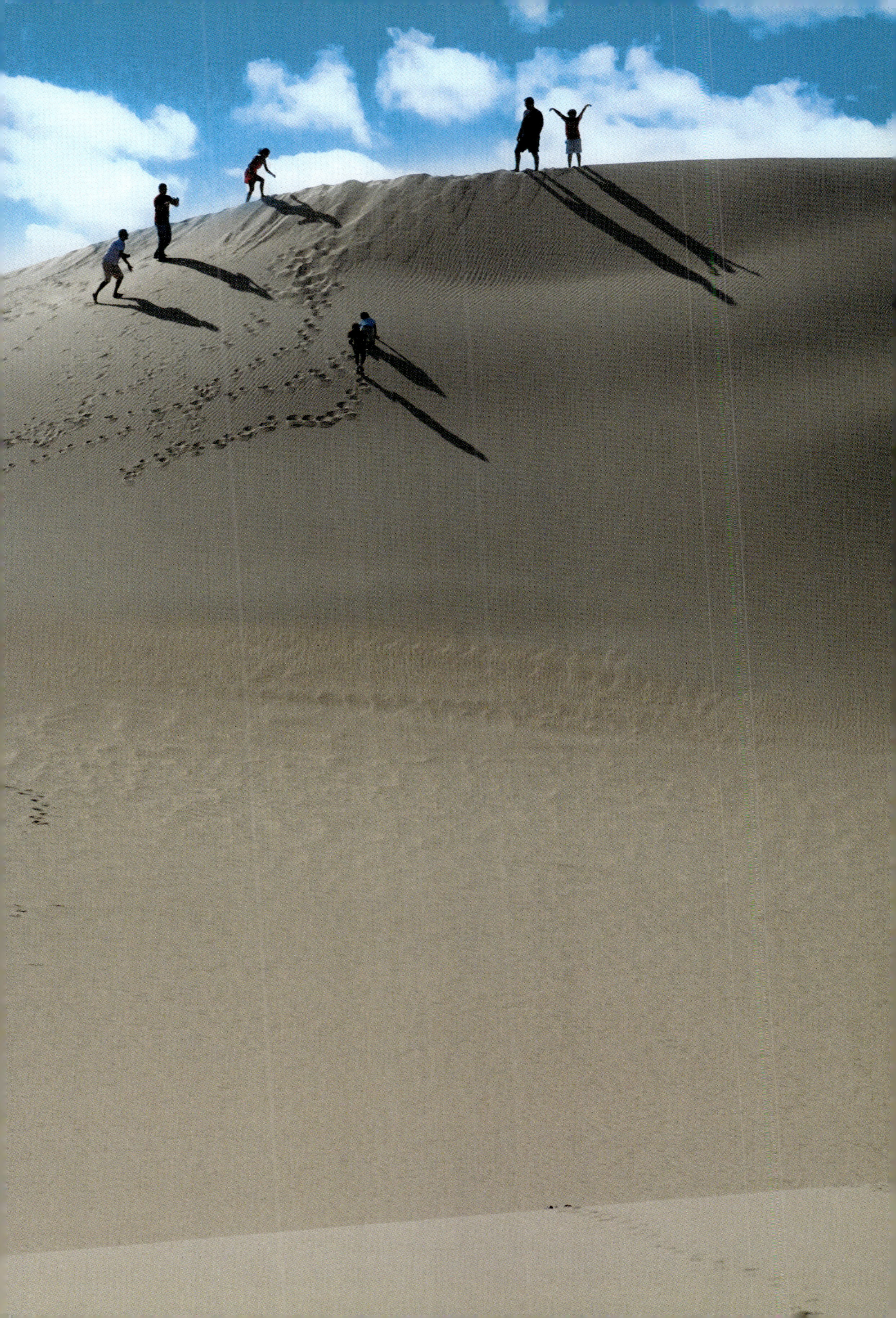

SOURCES & RECOMMENDED READING

BOOKS

Ahmed Fakhry, *Siwa Oasis*, The American University in Cairo Press, 1973

Philipp Vanderberg, *Mysteries of the Oracles*, Tauris Parke Paperbacks, 2007

Bahaa Taher, *Sunset Oasis*, Sceptre, 2009

Alain Blottiere, *Siwa: The Oasis*, Harpocrates Publishing, 2000

Azza Fahmy, *Enchanted Jewelry of Egypt*, The American University in Cairo Press, 2007

Michael Wood, *In the Footsteps of Alexander the Great*, BBC Books, 2004

MAGAZINES

W Magazine, June 2009

Condé Nast Traveller, April 2008

Vanity Fair, May 2007

New York Times Travel Supplement, Summer 2006

WEBSITES

http://en.wikipedia.org/wiki/Siwa_Oasis

http://www.siwa.com

http://edition.cnn.com/CNNI/Programs/middle.east

ABOUT THE CHARITY

Proceeds from this book will be directed to fund initiatives in Siwa in one or more of the following areas:

Education

Health

Culture

The Arts

This work will be part of SODIC's commitment to corporate social responsibility.

Please visit **www.sodic.com/csr/bookseries** for further information and regular updates.

SODIC

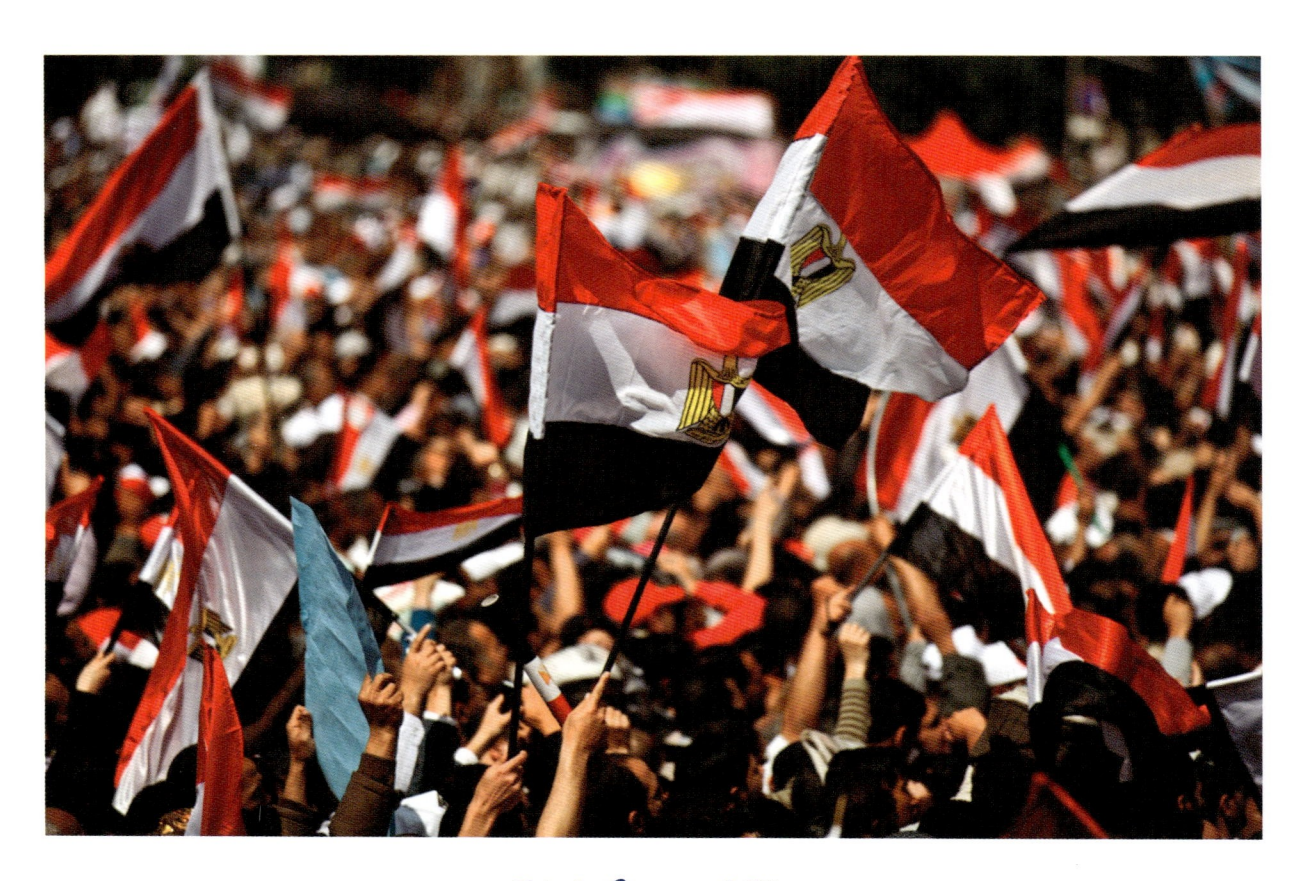

Tahrir Square, 2011

ACKNOWLEDGMENTS

THE BOOK TEAM ACKNOWLEDGES THAT AT THE TIME OF PRODUCING THIS BOOK, EGYPT UNDERWENT A PEACEFUL REVOLUTION THAT STARTED ON JANUARY 25TH, 2011, AND RESULTED IN THE FALL OF THE REGIME. THE WORLD WITNESSED EGYPTIANS FROM ALL WALKS OF LIFE AND BACKGROUNDS CONGREGATE DAILY OVER AN 18-DAY PERIOD IN TAHRIR SQUARE IN PEACEFUL PROTEST, DEMANDING FREEDOM AND DEMOCRACY. WE WERE VERY TOUCHED BY THIS MOMENTOUS TIME, AND COULD NOT BE MORE PROUD TO BE A PART OF IT IN SOME WAY.

AHEAD OF OUR PERSONAL ACKNOWLEDGEMENTS, THEREFORE, WE WOULD LIKE TO PAY TRIBUTE TO THE MEN AND WOMEN WHO LOST THEIR LIVES IN THE STRUGGLE FOR FREEDOM. MAY THEY FOREVER REST IN PEACE.

RAWAH ALFALAH BADRAWI

So many people stepped forward to lend their support to this book from the very beginning.

I would like to thank Dania Shawwa Abuali at Haven Books for her thoughtful mentoring. Design director Timothy Jones did a fantastic job of turning the raw material into the book we always dreamed of.

This endeavour would not have been possible without the critical intellectual and technical support provided by Dr Mounir Neamatalla, whose incredible work in Siwa has transformed lives and habitats.

His team in Siwa and Cairo supported us every step of the way, and I will never forget their kindness. We were fortunate enough to have the backing of SODIC, our corporate sponsor, whose real estate projects are game-changers in Egypt.

Finally, words cannot express my gratitude for the loving support of my family. My wonderful parents filled my room with books from a very young age and showed us the world.

My husband Dasha, who brought me to Egypt in 2001 to start a new life together. I dedicate this book to you and our three precious children Faris, Lina and Ziad.

OMAR HIKAL

I would like to extend a warm message of gratitude to all those who helped make this book not only a possibility, but a pleasure.

The fabulous team at Adrere Amellal:

Abdallah "Gasaa" Omar Abdallah,
Abdallah "Hamada" Moh. Youssef,
Mohamed Abdel Ader,
Abdelkarim Moh. Abdelkarim Ahmed,
Fagri Osman "Khaled" Abdallah Moh.,
Ibrahim "Gega" Mahmoud El-Sayed,
Ibrahim Moh. Ebeid,
Omar Moh. Ebeid,
and Saeed Ali Saeed.

Dr Mounir Neamatalla, for introducing us to Siwa.

My good friend Hussein Gohar for helping keep photography fun.

Khaled for bringing a fantastic light-heartedness and sense of humour along with some beautiful images to this project.

Rawah for making all this happen; for taking an embryo of an idea and seeing it through.

To my wife, Marine, for putting up with the hours of shooting and processing time, and for always being there. I dedicate this to you.

KHALED SHOKRY

Working on this book has been a great collaborative effort.

I want to thank Dina Abaza for assisting us in art direction, not an easy proposition when most of the time we shot in places with no electricity!

Dr Mounir Neamatalla was a kind and generous host; his staff were fantastic.

A special thanks to Yousry Zaghow.

A very special acknowledgement to my parents who encouraged me to save up for my first Canon A1 at the age of 12. Since then my interest in photography, travel, nature and cultures began.

Thank you for sowing those seeds. I dedicate the images I captured in Siwa to you as a gesture of eternal gratitude.

THE AUTHOR & PHOTOGRAPHERS

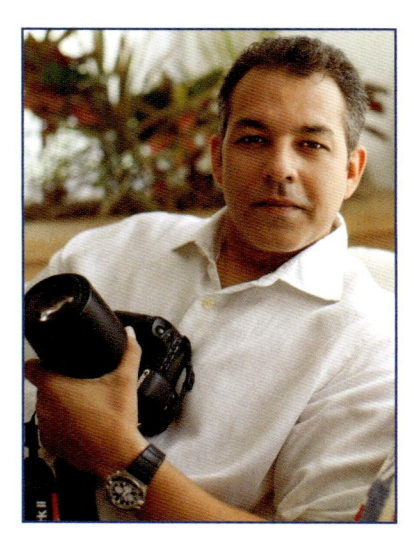

RAWAH ALFALAH BADRAWI is a Kuwaiti investment banker and freelance writer. She graduated with a B.S.c in Economics from Georgetown University and worked on Wall Street for several years before moving to London in 1998 and finally Cairo in 2001. Rawah is an enthusiastic traveler, constantly inspired by different cultures and lifestyles. The idea for this book originated after a special trip to Siwa in 2009. She was so moved by Siwa's beauty, proud people and advocates that she developed the idea of 'giving back' with her partners and sponsors, marking the start of her commitment to philanthropy and community service. Rawah lives in Sakkara, Egypt, with her husband and three children.

OMAR HIKAL is an entrepreneur and photography enthusiast. He graduated with a B.S.c in Business Administration from Boston University and worked extensively in the United States, and later the UAE and Egypt. He is co-founder and CEO of Archimedia ME, one of the region's most sophisticated residential technologies companies. He visited Siwa in October 2009, fell in love with the oasis town, and shot some of the photos that led to the idea of a book that would introduce Siwa to the world, and provide much needed funds to Siwan charities. He lives in Cairo, Egypt with his wife Marine. They have four children.

KHALED SHOKRY is a landscape designer, horticulturist and photographer. He graduated from Universite Paris IX Dauphine with an M.B.A. In subsequent years he worked in Europe and Egypt in various sectors, including food and beverage, construction and engineering, and design and architecture. In 1998 he founded the Palm Gardens, a multi-disciplinary firm that covers residential and corporate projects, from concept design to turn-key service. Khaled is a keen traveler, passionate cook and nature lover. He spends his time mainly between Cairo, his farm Botanica just outside the city, and the Far East.